Study Guide

for use with

Contemporary Management

Second Edition

Gareth Jones
Texas A&M University

Jennifer George
Texas A&M University

Charles Hill
University of Washington

Prepared by
Ernest King
University of Southern Mississippi

Irwin McGraw-Hill

Boston   Burr Ridge, IL   Dubuque, IA   Madison, WI   New York   San Francisco   St. Louis
Bangkok   Bogotá   Caracas   Lisbon   London   Madrid
Mexico City   Milan   New Delhi   Seoul   Singapore   Sydney   Taipei   Toronto

McGraw-Hill Higher Education

A Division of The McGraw·Hill Companies

Study Guide for use with
CONTEMPORARY MANAGEMENT

Copyright © 2000
by The McGraw-Hill Companies, Inc. All rights reserved.
Printed in the United States of America.

1 2 3 4 5 6 7 8 9 0 BKM/BKM 9 0 9 8 7 6 5 4 3 2 1 0 9

ISBN 0-07-233456-8

http://www.mhhe.com

CONTENTS

Chapter 1: Managers and Managing
    Journal Entries 1
    Chapter Outline 2
    Study Questions 4
    Video Case 8

Chapter 2: The Evolution of Management Theory
    Journal Entries 11
    Chapter Outline 12
    Study Questions 14
    Video Case 18

Chapter 3: The Organizational Environment
    Journal Entries 23
    Chapter Outline 24
    Study Questions 25
    Video Case (See Chapter 4, page 35— chapters 3 & 4 combined)

Chapter 4: The Global Environment
    Journal Entries 29
    Chapter Outline 30
    Study Questions 31
    Video Case 35

Chapter 5: Ethics, Social Responsibility, and Diversity
    Journal Entries 39
    Chapter Outline 40
    Study Questions 41
    Video Case 46

Chapter 6: The Manager as a Decision Maker
    Journal Entries 49
    Chapter Outline 50
    Study Questions 51
    Video Case 55

Chapter 7: The Manager as a Planner and Strategist
    Journal Entries 59
    Chapter Outline 60
    Study Questions 61
    Video Case 65

Chapter 8: Managing Organizational Structure
    Journal Entries 69
    Chapter Outline 70
    Study Questions 71
    Video Case 75

Chapter 9: Organizational Control and Culture
     Journal Entries 79
     Chapter Outline 80
     Study Questions 81
     Video Case 85

Chapter 10: Human Resources Management
     Journal Entries 89
     Chapter Outline 90
     Study Questions 91
     Video Case 96

Chapter 11: The Manager as a Person
     Journal Entries 99
     Chapter Outline 100
     Study Questions 101
     Video Case (No Video Case)

Chapter 12: Motivation
     Journal Entries 105
     Chapter Outline 106
     Study Questions 107
     Video Case 111

Chapter 13: Leadership
     Journal Entries 115
     Chapter Outline 116
     Study Questions 117
     Video Case 121

Chapter 14: Groups and Teams
     Journal Entries 125
     Chapter Outline 126
     Study Questions 127
     Video Case 132

Chapter 15: Communication
     Journal Entries 137
     Chapter Outline 138
     Study Questions 139
     Video Case 143

Chapter 16: Organizational Conflict, Negotiation, Politics, and Change
     Journal Entries 145
     Chapter Outline 146
     Study Questions 147
     Video Case 151

Chapter 17: Managing Information Systems and Technologies
     Journal Entries 155
     Chapter Outline 156
     Study Questions 157
     Video Case 161

Chapter 18: Operations Management: Managing Quality, Efficiency, and
             Responsiveness to Customers
      Journal Entries 163
      Chapter Outline.. 164
      Study Questions 165
      Video Case.. 169

Chapter 19: The Management of Innovation, Product Development,
             and Entrepreneurship
      Journal Entries 171
      Chapter Outline.. 172
      Study Questions 173
      Video Case (See Chapter 7, page 65—chapters 7 & 19 combined)

Concluding Journal Entry 177

Answers to the Study Questions 178

Journal Entries
Introduction

One of the goals of taking a principles of management course is to provide you, the student, with the opportunity to learn about the fundamentals of management theory and practice. However, unless you've been in the workforce for a period of time, some concepts might be hard to relate to or understand.

Karen Eboch of Bowling Green State University has written the following "Journal Entries" to help you apply what you are learning in the text to real-life situations. Each chapter of the text has 1-2 corresponding Journal Entries in the Study Guide with questions you answer based on experiences you may have had or are having in your life. You can use a notebook to answer the questions from the Study Guide, or you can use the electronic files found on the CD-Rom. You should be able to cut & paste the questions from the CD-Rom into whatever word-processing program you are using, and type the answers to the questions.

Your professor might choose to assign as homework, but this is also a good way to check your progress after completing a chapter.

Journal Entries
Chapter 1 - Managers and Managing

Entry 1:
1. What types of organizations do you belong to? How do they meet the 3 criteria of organizations?
2. What do you "manage?" How efficient and/or effective are you?
3. How do you use the four managerial processes to manage your life?
4. Which of the four managerial processes does your boss emphasize (current, past, expected future)?
5. What types of skills should you emphasize in interviews for your first job after graduation? Why?

Entry 2:
1. Is/was your boss able to portray all 10 roles? Which was he/she better at? Which did he/she tend not to perform?
2. How do the managerial challenges impact your professional career choices?

Chapter 1

Managers and Managing

Chapter Outline

I. Steve Jobs's Old and New Management Styles
    A. Conflict Among Employees
    B. Lack of Vision
    C. Clear Leadership
    D. Effective Planning

II. Chapter Overview

III. What is Management
    A. Utilization of Resources
    B. Achieving Goals
        1. Organizational performance
        2. Efficiency
        3. Effectiveness
    C. Management Insight - How to be an Effective Plant Manager
        1. Accessability
        2. Feedback

IV. Managerial Functions
    A. Planning
        1. Deciding goals
        2. Deciding courses of action
        3. Allocating resources
        4. Developing a strategy
    B. Organizing
        1. Grouping people by tasks
        2. Establishing authority
        3. Establishing responsibility
    C. Leading
        1. Using power and influence
        2. Articulating vision
        3. Communicating effectively
    D. Controlling
        1. Monitoring individuals and departments
        2. Monitoring the organization as a whole
        3. Maintaining standards

V.   Types of Managers
        A.   First-line Managers (Supervisors)
        B.   Middle Managers
        C.   Top Managers
        D.   Job Specific Skills

VI.   Recent Changes in Managerial Hierarchies
        A.   Restructuring
                1.   Downsizing
                2.   Promoting efficiency through cost reduction
        B.   Empowerment and Self-Management Teams
        C.   Management insight - A New Approach at John Deere
                1.   Direct customer contact
                2.   Extensive training

VII.   Managerial Roles and Skills
        A.   Interpersonal Roles
                1.   Figurehead
                2.   Leader
                3.   Liaison
        B.   Informational Roles
                1.   Monitor
                2.   Disseminator
                3.   Spokesperson
        C.   Decisional Roles
                1.   Entrepreneur
                2.   Disturbance handler
                3.   Resource allocator
                4.   Negotiator
        D.   Management Insight - Effective Small Business Management

VIII.   Being a Manager

IX.   Managerial Skills
        A.   Concept Skills
                1.   Formal education and training
                2.   Specialized programs
        B.   Human Skills
                1.   Education and training
                2.   Experience
        C.   Technical Skills

X.   Challenges for Management In a Global Environment
        A.   Building a Competitive Advantage
        B.   Increasing Efficiency

C.   Increasing Quality
D.   Increasing Innovation
E.   Increasing Responsiveness to Customers
F.   Managing Globally - How Levi Strauss Built an International Competitive Advantage
G.   Maintaining Ethical Standards
H.   Ethics in Action - How to Destroy a Charity's Reputation
I.   Managing a Diverse Workforce
J.   Focus on Diversity - Making the Most of Difference
K.   Utilizing New information Systems and Technology
L.   Management Insight - The Information Revolution at Hewlett - Packard

Study Questions

True - False Questions

___ 1.   Resources are assets such as people, machinery, and information.

___ 2.   Organizational performance increases in inverse proportion to increases in efficiency and effectiveness.

___ 3.   Effectiveness is a measure of how well or how productively resources are used to achieve a goal.

___ 4.   Fayol first outlined the nature of managerial activities around the turn of the nineteenth century.

___ 5.   Managers at all levels and in all departments of for-profit, but not non-profit, organizations are responsible for performing all four managerial functions.

___ 6.   Organizational structure determines how an organization's resources can best be used to create goods and services.

___ 7.   The outcome of leadership is a high level of motivation and commitment among organizational members.

___ 8.   Within each department are all three levels of management.

___ 9.   Top managers are increasingly encouraging lower-level managers to take a cross-departmental view of the business.

___ 10.   Restructuring can produce some highly negative outcomes.

Multiple Choice Questions

_____ 1.   Management involves which of these to achieve organizational goals:

        I.   Planning
        II.   Leading
        III.   Organizing
        IV.   Consistency

    A.   I, II, III
    B.   II, III, IV
    C.   I, II, IV
    D.   I, II, III, IV

_____ 2.   Organizations are efficient when managers:

        I.   Maximize the amount of inputs
        II.   Minimize the time needed for production
        III.   Minimize the time needed for services rendered

    A.   II and III
    B.   I and II
    C.   I and III
    D.   I, II, and III

_____ 3.   Which is **not** a step in the planning process:
    A.   Deciding on organizational goals
    B.   Deciding on actions to pursue
    C.   Allocating resources to attain goals
    D.   Performance appraisal

_____ 4.   The outcome of planning is a(n) _____.
    A.   performance
    B.   strategy
    C.   assessment
    D.   effective organization

_____ 5.   Which statement is **false** concerning organizing?
    A.   It is a process managers use to establish the structure of working relationships.
    B.   It involves grouping people into departments based on undifferentiated tasks they perform.
    C.   It lays out lines of authority and responsibility.
    D.   Managers decide how best to coordinate organizational resources.

_____ 6.   The outcome of the _____ process is the ability to measure performance accurately and regulate organizational efficiency and effectiveness.
    A.   assessment
    B.   leading

C.   control

D.   effectiveness

___ 7.   First-line managers are also known as:

A.   front-line managers.

B.   middle managers.

C.   supervisors.

D.   top managers.

___ 8.   Who has the responsibility to find the best way to organize human resources to achieve organizational goals?

A.   First-line managers

B.   Middle managers

C.   Top managers

D.   Supervisors

___ 9.   Top managers:

    I.   Establish departmental goals

    II.   Decide how different companies should interact

    III.   Monitor how well first-line managers utilize resources

A.   I and II

B.   II and III

C.   I, II, and III

D.   None of these

___ 10.   Corporations today typically employ about ___% fewer managers than they did 10 years ago.

A.   5

B.   10

C.   20

D.   15

___ 11.   Which of these should reduce costs and improve quality:

    I.   Empowerment of the workforce

    II.   Limiting employees' responsibilities

    III.   Creation of self-managed teams

A.   I and III

B.   I only

C.   II and III

D.   III only

___ 12.   Which of these is **not** a Mintzberg category of roles for managers?

A.   Interpersonal

B.   Informational

C.   Motivational

D.   Decisional

___ 13.   A manager's first interpersonal role is to act as a:

A.   figurehead.

B.   leader.

C.   liaison.

D.   monitor.

___ 14.   Which of these is **not** an informational role?

A.   Monitor

B.   Spokesperson

C.   Disseminator

D.   Liaison

___ 15.   Research has shown that education and experience help managers acquire all but which one of these types of skills:

A.   Technical

B.   Human

C.   Linguistic

D.   Conceptual

Essay Questions

1.   Why is planning a difficult activity for a manager?

2.   What main items do managers perform when they lead?

3.   Why did Michael Dell have difficulty establishing effective control systems?

4.   What are the challenges for management in the competitive global environment?

Chapter 1
Managers and Managing
featuring United Airlines

This video focuses on the management style of United Airlines whose headquarters is just outside of Chicago, Illinois. It looks at the company's recent change to becoming employee-owned and what effect that has had on management philosophy as it relates to quality and competitiveness.

On July 12, 1994 United Airlines became the world's largest employee-owned company. In their new role as owners and investors, employees must take advantage of this distinction to position the company for long-term competitiveness in the airline industry. The new owners are working to create a new organizational culture that fosters high commitment to employee involvement, open and honest communication, sharing of ideas, trust, respect for diversity, and teamwork.

One innovation already developed by the new owners is "Customer Problem Resolution teams," a new customer-satisfaction initiative. These teams illustrate the point that, in order to be successful in an intensely competitive global environment, UAL feels it can no longer operate in the traditional ways of having only management involved in the business. Because United is an employee-owned company, now more than ever, it needs the commitment of ideas and the decision malting of each "owner" in order to become world class competitors.

UAL's new management style views employee participation, customer focus, and continuous improvement as essential factors to its success and profitability. Management is confronted with the task of becoming more involved in encouraging and empowering employees to solve problems immediately, by themselves. In this regard they have instituted several aggressive new programs emanating from their Culture Change division.

The overarching campaign of this new management approach is their Mission United program. Basically this is a one day event for all employees for the purpose of gaining an understanding of how they must work together differently in achieving their primary goal: To become the worldwide airline of choice.

Each Mission United event is planned for approximately 150 employees that are mixed from all departments, levels, and job group within the company. The enrollment process is designed to insure a maximum mix of employee job groups as well as a cross-function of departments and divisions at each event. At Mission United events, each participant is challenged to:

- Become thoroughly acquainted with United's mission, vision and values;
- Gain a better understanding of how business decisions are made;
- Heighten awareness of their individual impact on the customer,
- Take a look at the strengths and weaknesses of the company;

- Inter-act with fellow employees;
- Examine the concept of ownership; and
- Share breakthrough successes and learn how employees are working differently.

Through Mission United, employees are oriented to focus on the company's 'core values' of teamwork, safety, integrity, respect, community service, customer satisfaction, and profitability. Basically, the company feels that these values are going to help them achieve their goal 'to be the worldwide airline of choice," with the top priority of providing a safe airline.

As an outgrowth of this new kind of management approach to employee involvement United has instituted a new employee participation process to focus on customer service, organizational concerns, and profitability. Taking the best practices from the most successful companies with high commitment to employee involvement they created the "Best of Best" process. The main thrust of this process involves employees working together in teams to identify and resolve local operational and quality issues which impact the customer. The focus of Best of Best teams is for continuous improvement of services within the boundaries of the team's control. Teams will have a clear understanding of their goals and are empowered at the local level to work on creative new ways of doing business.

The Best of Best program was the first attempt by United to bridge all divisions together to solve problems. It represents the beginning of a long-term cultural transformation to a collaborative, decision-making, learning organization in which employees are encouraged to gain new skills and work differently. Teamwork is valued and rewarded, responsibility and accountability are maximized, personal and professional growth are continuous, and hierarchy is minimized. Self-determination, self-motivation, and self-management are expected, and management is providing the leadership necessary to drive and sustain the empowerment.

Managers have become more visible to the United employees as well. They are making it a point to spend time on the front lines of the business in order to do a better job leading and planning for culture change. In many cases, they are leading by doing and are certainly much more open and available to their employees than they were in the past. The managers have been conducting "road shows" that become interactive question-and-answer sessions to encourage open communication with staff members.

Since becoming an employee-owned company, United Airlines has had to do a lot of internal soul searching to discover a better way of doing things. This major cultural change has served to accelerate the company's strategic shift to becoming more competitive on a global scale. Fortunately, as owners they were forced to focus on new and dynamic ways of doing things. They realized that exceeding the customer's expectations is the only way to compete and achieve their goals. By turning to greater employee involvement and more responsive management, they appear to be headed in the right direction.

QUESTIONS FOR REVIEW AND DISCUSSION

1. United Airlines managers use an approach called Mission United to orient employees throughout the organization to new initiatives, goals, and competitive position. Discuss in class how managers should conduct these one-day sessions to get maximum employee buy-in and commitment.

2. Best of Best programs are cross-functional teams aimed at creating changes based on identified best practices. Why do you think United organized these teams cross-functionally?

3. Employee ownership has been attempted before in the airline industry through a company called People Express. That company didn't survive, although it was initially successful. What are some steps UAL can take to improve its chances of success?

Journal Entries
Chapter 2 - The Evolution of Management Theory

Entry 3:
1. How would you apply the four principles of Scientific Management to the job of student?
2. Is your university a bureaucracy? Explain using the elements identified by Weber.
3. Does your employer/university apply all 14 of Fayol's principles of management? Which are best used? Which ones are missing?

Entry 4:
1. Which management view do you agree with most? Why?
2. Which management view does your manager/a professor seem to favor? Explain.
3. What else do you see happening to management theories in the next 20 years?
4. Describe two similar situations that didn't turn out the same. What was different and how did that difference impact the outcome.
5. Describe the structure of your family or work place. Is it more organic or mechanistic?

Chapter 2

The Evolution of Management Theory

Chapter Outline

I.   Changing Ways of Making Cars
    A.   Small Batch Production
    B.   Mass Production Manufacturing
    C.   Lean Manufacturing

II.   Chapter Overview

III.   Scientific Management Theory
    A.   Impact of the Industrial Revolution
    B.   Job Specialization and Division of Labor
    C.   F. W. Taylor and Scientific Management
        1.   Study performance and experiment with improvements
        2.   Codify methods of performance into written rules and standard operating procedures
        3.   Match skills of workers to the needs of the task and train to follow rules and procedures
        4.   Establish acceptable levels of performance and monetarily reward performance above that level
    D.   Ethics in Action - Fordism In Practice
    E.   The Gilbreths
        1.   Time and motion studies
        2.   Fatigue

IV.   Administrative Management Theory
    A.   The Theory of Bureaucracy
        1.   A manager's formal authority is derived from the manager's position in the organization
        2.   People should occupy positions based on performance
        3.   The extent of formal authority and responsibility should be clearly specified
        4.   Positions should be arranged hierarchically
        5.   Managers must create a well-defined system of rules and procedures to effectively maintain control
    B.   Fayol's Principles of Management
        1.   Division of labor
        2.   Authority and responsibility
        3.   Unity of command
        4.   Line of authority

        5.   Centralization
        6.   Unity of direction
        7.   Equity
        8.   Order
        9.   Initiative
        10.   Discipline
        11.   Remuneration of personnel
        12.   Stability of tenure of personnel
        13.   Subordination of individual interests to the common interest
        14.   Esprit de corps
    C.   Management insight - How to be an Excellent Company

V.   Behavioral Management Theory
    A.   The Work of Mary Parker Follett
        1.   Cross-functioning
        2.   Fluidity of power
    B.   The Hawthorne Studies and Human Relations
        1.   Relay assembly test requirements
        2.   Hawthorne effect
        3.   Human relations training
        4.   Informal organization's impact
    C.   Theory X
    D.   Theory Y
    E.   Theory Z
    F.   Management Insight - The Hewlett - Packard Way

VI.   Management Science Theory
    A.   Quantitative Management
    B.   Operations Management
    C.   Total Quality Management (TQM)
    D.   Management Information Systems

VII.   Organizational Environment Theory
    A.   The Open-Systems View
        1.   Input stage
        2.   Conversion stage
        3.   Output stage
    B.   Contingency Theory
        1.   Mechanistic structure
        2.   Organic structure
    C.   Managing Globally - Phillips's Organic Structure Works

Study Questions

True - False Questions

____ 1.   Scientific management theory was the earliest of the management theories.

____ 2.   Theories such as TQM are often viewed as advances of early scientific management theories.

____ 3.   Bureaucracy is a formal system of organization and administration designed to ensure efficiency and effectiveness.

____ 4.   Standard operating procedures are written, informal codes of conduct that prescribe behaviors.

____ 5.   Discipline is the methodical arrangement of positions to provide the greatest benefit to the organization.

____ 6.   Esprit de corps is a shared feeling of enthusiasm or a devotion to a common cause by members of a group.

____ 7.   Theory X has negative assumptions about workers.

____ 8.   Theory Y is an approach to management that recognizes and rewards individual achievements within a group context.

____ 9.   A closed system is self-contained and not affected changes in the internal environment.

____ 10.   An organic structure is one in which authority is centralized, rules are specified, and employees are closely supervised.

Multiple Choice Questions

____ 1.   Who is a person who advanced early scientific management principles?
           A.   Weber
           B.   Taylor
           C.   Vest
           D.   Fayol

____ 2.   Which worked on administrative management theory:
                          I.   Fayol
                          II.   Parker
                          III.   Weber
           A.   I and III
           B.   II and III

C. I and III
D. I, II, and III

___ 3.   _____ is the study of how to create an organizational structure that leads to high efficiency and effectiveness.
A. Scientific management
B. Job specialization
C. Administrative management
D. Allocation management

___ 4.   A reporting relationship in which an employee receives orders from, and reports to, only one supervisor is known as:
A. line of authority.
B. centralization.
C. unity of direction.
D. unity of command.

___ 5.   _____ is the singleness of purpose that makes possible the creation of one plan of action to guide managers in resource allocations.
A. Unity of direction
B. Unity of command
C. Unity of authority
D. Unity of resources

___ 6.   Which is an organizational - environmental theory?
        I.   The open-systems view
        II. Contingency theory
        III. The Theory of Bureaucracy
        IV. Theory Z
A. I and II
B. I, III, and IV
C. II, III, and IV
D. I, II, and III

___ 7.   The _____ effect is the finding that a manager's behavior or leadership approach can affect workers' level of performance.
A. Henthorne
B. Hawthorne
C. Follett
D. Fayol

___ 8.   Theory __ is based on positive assumptions about workers.
A. Z
B. X
C. Y

D.   C

___ 9.   A(n) _____ system takes resources from its external environment and converts them into goods and services for customer purchase.
A.   closed
B.   free
C.   semi-open
D.   open

___ 10.   _____ is the tendency of a system to lose its ability to control itself and thus disintegrate.
A.   Empathy
B.   Entropy
C.   Synergy
D.   Chaos

___ 11.   The _____ theory states a manager's choice of organizational structures and control systems depends on characteristics of the external environment.
A.   mechanistic
B.   management science
C.   organic
D.   contingency

___ 12.   Which is **not** one of Fayol's principles:
A.   Authority and responsibility
B.   Line of authority
C.   Globalization
D.   Unity of command

___ 13.   Which is **not** a management science theory:
A.   Operations management
B.   TQM
C.   MIS
D.   None of these

___ 14.   Theory __ states that the average employee is lazy and will try to do as little as possible.
A.   X
B.   Y
C.   Z
D.   None

___ 15.   Which is **not** part of the input stage of an open system?
A.   Raw materials
B.   Human resources

C. Computers
D. Money and capital

Essay Questions

1. Why is esprit de corps valuable to a business?

2. Compare and contrast Theory X and Theory Y.

3. Why is unity of command important?

4. Why cab long-term employees improve organizational efficiency?

Chapter 2
The Evolution of Management

The management profession, as we know it today, is relatively new, even though the issues and problems that confront managers have existed for thousands of years. Management emerged as a formal discipline at the turn of the century, when rapid industrialization called for better-skilled management of natural resources, capital, and labor. The various management approaches that have been developed can be divided into two major groups: classical approaches and contemporary approaches.

The classical approaches, which extended from the mid-19th century through the early 1950s, emerged as managers tried to cope with the growth of American industry. These approaches were systematic management, scientific management, administrative management, human relations, and bureaucracy.

Systematic management represented the beginning of formal management thought in the U.S. It emphasized the way in which manufacturing firms operated because most management problems were focused on manufacturing.

Scientific management was introduced around the turn of the century by Frederick Taylor, an engineer who applied scientific methods to analyze work and determine the "one best way" to complete production tasks. Taylor stressed the importance of hiring and training the proper workers to do those tasks. One of the most famous examples of the application of scientific management is the factory Henry Ford built to produce the Model T. Ford's use of scientific management principles yielded higher productivity and efficiency. For example, by 1914, chassis assembly time had been trimmed from almost 13 hours to 1.5 hours.

Administrative management emerged at about the same time and emphasized the perspective of senior managers within the organization. It viewed management as a profession that could be taught.

The human relations approach to management evolved from the Hawthorne studies conducted from 1924 to 1932 at the Western Electric Company outside Chicago. Various working conditions, particularly lighting, were altered to determine the effects of these changes on productivity. But researchers, led by Harvard professor Elton Mayo, were ultimately unable to determine any relationship between factory lighting and productivity levels. This led the researchers to believe the productivity was affected more by psychological and social factors. This approach highlighted the importance of the human element in the organization. However, critics believed the human relations philosophy of "the happy worker as a productive worker" was too simplistic.

Max Weber, a German sociologist and social historian, developed the bureaucratic approach to management. He attempted to establish an overall management system by focusing on a structured, formal network of relationships among specialized positions in an organization. Bureaucracy allowed efficient performance of many routine activities. The contemporary approaches to management, which have been developed since World War II, attempted to overcome the limitations of the classical approaches. The contemporary approaches include quantitative management, organizational behavior, systems theory, and the contingency perspective.

Quantitative management was aided by the development of modern computers. It emphasizes the application of a formal, mathematical model to management decisions and problems.
The organizational behavior approach to management promotes employee effectiveness through an understanding of the complex nature of individual, group, and organizational processes.
The systems theory of management, which originated in the 195-s, was a major effort to overcome the limitations of the earlier approaches by attempting to view, the organizations as a whole system. Systems theory introduced the concept of equifinality— that there is no "one best way" to reach a goal. And it stresses the notion of synergy—that the whole is greater than the sum of its parts.

The contingency perspective has most recently dominated the study of management. It asserts that situational characteristics, or contingencies, determine the management strategies that will be most effective. This approach argues that no universal principle should *always* be applied. Rather, managers, like those at Trek Bicycle, analyze situations and then, based on their analysis of key contingencies, make decisions regarding the most appropriate ways to manage. Trek, based in rural Wisconsin, has a very open-minded approach to managing, and meeting customer needs.

But the evolution of management doesn't end there. Management thought and practice continues to evolve. Current events and trends are shaping the future of business and of management. Among the major forces now revolutionizing management are: globalization, learning organization, total quality management, and reengineering.

Globalization refers to the rise of multinational enterprises in the ever-expanding global marketplace. Even small firms that don't operate on a global scale must make important strategic decisions based on international considerations. Trek Bicycle recently discovered the importance of the global market In the mid 1980s, only a small percent of its revenues came from foreign sales. However, as international sales manager Joyce Keehn said, "When we began to get into other markets like Germany and Japan their standards were much higher than what we were experiencing here in the states. So, in effect, these countries helped us increase our quality because we wanted to grow our business in these countries we listened to what the dealers and the market was expecting from us and we implemented those quality changes here." Today, Trek sells its bicycles in 55 countries with international sales accounting for 40 percent of its business.

The learning organization is committed to openness, new ideas, generating new knowledge, and spreading information and knowledge to others. Continuing dialogue and open-mindedness with an eye toward achieving the organization's goals is the foremost concern. Tellabs, Chicago-area manufacturer of telecommunications products and services, is a learning organization that has emphasized innovation, teams, and mentoring. It seems to be working. Tellabs stock has increased by more than 1,600 percent over the last five years, outperforming every other publicly traded stock in the nation. Tellabs employee Eric Bean said, "My experience with mentoring has been phenomenal. My life has completely changed by the inputs of other people."

Total quality management, or TQM, refers to an approach to management that produces customer satisfaction by providing high quality goods and services. Its goal is to solve and then eliminate all quality-related problems. First National Bank of Chicago has an aggressive quality program that includes weekly performance review meetings. In the meetings, managers analyze dozens of charts that are designed to monitor the quality of their performance.

First National's Rich Gilgan said, "You can't manage what you don't understand. And you don't understand what you don't measure. So measuring things is absolutely critical to understanding how our performance is improving or not improving, where we have problems. Because it's in that way that we can go back and identify what the root cause of those problems. So measures are absolutely critical."

Finally, business reengineering is the process of starting all over to rebuild the company and overhaul its *ways* of doing business. The goal of reengineering is to achieve dramatic improvements in critical perform measures including cost, quality innovation, and speed. Reengineering requires a way of thinking that's quite different from traditional management practices.

From the classical approaches, through the contemporary approaches, and into the forces now revolutionizing management, the history of past efforts, triumphs, and failures has become the guide to future management practice. Since the mid-19th century, change has been the constant in the evolution of management. The marketplace keeps changing, the technology keeps changing, and the work force keeps changing. Today's manager must learn how to deal with the forces of change affecting management Only by understanding the implications of change and the challenges it presents will you be prepared to meet them head-on.

CRITICAL THINKING QUESTIONS

1.   In general, how do contemporary approaches to management differ from classical approaches?

2.   What are some modern organizational problems that are a result of classical approaches to managing?

3.   The Hawthorne studies are frequently cited as a turning point in management thought. What is the significance of this research?

Journal Entries
Chapter 3 - The Organizational Environment

Entry 5:
1. Describe the elements of your task and general environment.
2. How does the environment impact you?
3. How can/do you impact the environment of a major organization?
4. Do you face barriers to entry? How do they relate to you and your "product life cycle?"
5. What boundaries do you span? How do you do it?
6. Describe the structure of your family or work place. Is it more organic or mechanistic?

Chapter 3

The Organizational Environment

Chapter Outline

I.   Personal Computers
     A.   Compaq's Ron Canion
     B.   Eckhard Pfeiffer

II. The Organizational Environment

III. The Task Environment
     A.   Suppliers
     B.   Distributors
     C.   Customers
     D.   Ethics in Action - Merck and Company Develops a Free Treatment for River Blindness
     E.   Competitors
     F.   Barriers to Entry
          1.   Economies of scale
          2.   Brand loyalty
     G.   Management Insight - It's Hard to Get into the Jet Business
     H.   The Industry Life Cycle
          1.   Birth
          2.   Growth
          3.   Shakeout
          4.   Maturity
          5.   Decline

IV. The General Environment
     A.   Economic Forces
     B.   Technological Forces
     C.   Management Insight - Computer-Aided Design Makes a Difference at Boeing
     D.   Socio-cultural Forces
          1.   Social structure
          2.   National culture
     E.   Demographic Forces
     F.   Political and Legal Forces
     G.   Global Forces

V.   Managing the Organizational Environment
     A.   Environmental Complexity and Rate of Change

B.   Reducing the Impact of Environmental Forces
C.   Creating an Organizational Structure and Control Systems
     1.   Mechanistic structure
     2.   Organic structure
     3.   Internal structure
D.   Boundary - Spanning Roles
     1.   Representing and protecting the organization
     2.   Scanning and monitoring the environment
     3.   Gatekeeping and information processing
     4.   Establishing Inter-organizational Relationships
E.   Managing Globally - T. Julie Berry Discovers China
F.   Managers as Agents of Change
G.   Management Insight - Bill Lowe Changes the Rules of the Game

Study Questions

<u>True - False Questions</u>

___ 1.   An organizational environment is the set of forces and conditions that operate inside an organization's boundaries that affect a manager's ability to acquire resources.

___ 2.   A task environment is the set of forces and conditions that originate with suppliers, distributors, customers, and competitors.

___ 3.   The general environment considers factors such as demographic, political, and legal forces on the organization.

___ 4.   Barriers to entry are illegal.

___ 5.   Economies of scale are factors that make it difficult and costly for a business to enter an environment.

___ 6.   Economic forces can be national or regional.

___ 7.   Socio-cultural forces are only local in focus.

___ 8.   The arrangement of relationships between individuals and groups in a society is called the socio-economic structure.

___ 9.   Boundary spanning is interacting with those outside of the organization to obtain information from the task and general environment.

___ 10.   Gatekeeping is deciding what information to allow and not allow into the organization.

Multiple Choice Questions

___ 1.   The _____ environment is the set of forces and conditions that operate beyond an organization's boundaries but affect the manager's ability to acquire and utilize resources.
  A.   organizational
  B.   task
  C.   general
  D.   socio-cultural

___ 2.   The _____ environment originates with, among others, customers and competitors.
  A.   organizational
  B.   task
  C.   general
  D.   socio-cultural

___ 3.   The general environment considers all but which of these forces:
  A.   Political
  B.   Demographic
  C.   Legal
  D.   Distributor-based

___ 4.   Who helps organizations sell their goods to customers?
  A.   Suppliers
  B.   Distributors
  C.   Customers
  D.   Competitors

___ 5.   Who provides necessary inputs for production for an organization?
  A.   Suppliers
  B.   Distributors
  C.   Customers
  D.   Competitors

___ 6.   Which is **not** a stage of an industry life cycle:
  A.   Growth
  B.   Seniority
  C.   Shakeout
  D.   Birth

___ 7.   Which is an economic force:
           A.   Interest rates
           B.   Inflation
           C.   Unemployment
           D.   All of the above

___ 8.   Managers utilize technological forces to affect:
                              I.   Distribution
                              II.   Production
                              III.   Design
           A.   III only
           B.   II and III
           C.   I, II, and III
           D.   I and III

___ 9.   Pressures emanating from society or the national culture are called _____ forces.
           A.   socio-economic
           B.   socio-cultural
           C.   bio-cultural
           D.   socio-technological

___ 10.   The arrangement of relationships between individuals and groups in a society is
           called the:
           A.   national culture.
           B.   demographic structure.
           C.   social structure
           D.   psychographic structure

___ 11.   The _____ culture is the set of values a society considers important.
           A.   national
           B.   global
           C.   local
           D.   regional

___ 12.   Which of the following is a demographic force?
                              I.   Age
                              II.   Gender
                              III.   Ethnicity
                              IV.   Social class
           A.   I, II, and III
           B.   I, III, and IV
           C.   II, III, and IV
           D.   I, II, III, and IV

___ 13.   By 1992, what percentage of working-age women were in the workforce?

A. 35
B. 50
C. 90
D. 72

___ 14.   _____ change is the degree to which forces in the task and general environment evolve over time.
A. Environmental
B. Technological
C. Organizational
D. Industrial

___ 15.   According to t he textbook, gatekeeping can _____ the quality of decision making.
A. clarify
B. focus
C. obscure
D. enhance

Essay Questions

1.   What are the components of the organizational environment?

2.   How do legal forces, such as environmental laws, pose an opportunity to managers?

3.   How is an organizational structure developed?

4.   What types of activities are included in boundary-spanning roles?

Journal Entries
Chapter 4 -The Global Environment

Entry 6:
1. How does globalization positively influence your life? How does globalization negatively impact you?
2. Within your lifetime, what do you think has been the most significant global change? Why?
3. If you (as a future graduate) are the product, what barriers to international trade do you face? What do your competitors face?
4. If you have traveled internationally, what was the most surprising difference you encountered?
5. Where would you fall in the Hofstede framework? Do you match the U.S.?
6. Describe the sociocultural differences you have observed or encountered due to the diversity of this university.
7. Will you work your entire career in one country? Over the course of your career, what changes do you expect to experience as a result of the changing international dynamics?

Chapter 4

The Global Environment

Chapter Outline

I.   The Limited and Toys'R'Us

II.   The Changing Global Environment
    A.   Declining Barriers to Trade and Investment
        1.   GATT and the rise of free trade
        2.   Free trade doctrine
    B.   Declining Barriers of Distance and Culture
    C.   Effects of Free Trade on Managers

III.   The Global Task Environment
    A.   Suppliers
    B.   Managing Globally - Swan Optical Spreads Its Wings
        1.   Global outsourcing
    C.   Distributors
    D.   Customers
    E.   Competitors

IV.   The Global General Environment
    A.   Political and Legal Forces
        1.   Representative democracies
        2.   Totalitarian regimes
    B.   Economic Forces
        1.   Free market economy
        2.   Command economy
    C.   Changes in Political, Legal, and Economic Forces
        1.   Failure of totalitarian regimes
        2.   Shift to free-market model
    D.   Managing Globally - G. E.'s U.S. Managers Stumble in Hungary
    E.   Socio-cultural Forces
        1.   Societal values
        2.   Norms
        3.   Mores
        4.   Hofstede's Model of National Culture
        5.   Individualism versus Collectivism
        6.   Power distance
            a.   High power distance
            b.   Low power distance

7.   Achievement versus nurturing orientation
8.   Uncertainty avoidance
9.   Long-term versus short-term orientation
10.   National culture and global management
11.   Culture shock

V.   Choosing a Way to Expand Internationally
     A.   Importing and Exporting
     B.   Licensing and Franchising
     C.   Strategic Alliances
           1.   Joint venture
     D.   Wholly Owned Foreign Subsidiaries
     E.   Managing Globally - How to Get the World Hooked on Fish and Chips

VI. Impediments to an Open Global Environment
     A.   Government-imposed Impediments
     B.   Managing Globally - Wal-Mart Runs into Red Tape
     C.   Self-Imposed Ethical Impediments
     D.   Ethics In Action - Anita Roddick's Fair-Trade Philosophy

Study Questions

<u>True - False Questions</u>

___ 1.   A tariff is a tax generally imposed on exported goods.

___ 2.   The idea that each country specializes in the production of the goods and services that it can most efficiently produce using its global resources is known as the free-trade doctrine.

___ 3.   A dictatorship is a political system in which a single party or group holds all political power and does not permit opposition.

___ 4.   A command economy is an economic system in which the government owns all the businesses and controls the markets.

___ 5.   Norms are ideas that society believes to be right.

___ 6.   Values are unwritten rules of conduct that dictate conduct.

___ 7.   Mores are central to the functioning of society.

___ 8.   Collectivism is a world view that values the group over the individual.

31

___ 9.   The world view that values the quality of life is called the natural orientation.

___ 10.   A joint venture is a strategic alliance among two or more corporations that agree to jointly establish and share ownership of a newly created business.

Multiple Choice Questions

___ 1.   A _____ organization is one that operates and competes in more than one country.
   A.   universal
   B.   global
   C.   international
   D.   multi-national

___ 2.   Which of the following is **not** a reason for global outsourcing:
   A.   The purchase of global inputs from foreign suppliers
   B.   Production of inputs abroad
   C.   Lower production costs
   D.   Lower quality or designs

___ 3.   A _____ economy is an economic system in which private enterprise controls production and the interaction of supply and demand determines price and quantity of the goods.
   A.   free-market
   B.   command
   C.   mixed
   D.   totalitarian

___ 4.   An economic system that combines private ownership and governmental mechanisms is known as a _____ economy.
   A.   command
   B.   combination
   C.   mixed
   D.   hybrid

___ 5.   The set of values that society considers important and the approved norms of behavior are known as the _____ culture.
   A.   national
   B.   international
   C.   local
   D.   regional

___ 6.   The ideas and beliefs that a society believes to be good and desirable are called:
   A.   norms.
   B.   values.
   C.   folkways

D.   mores.

___ 7.   These are unwritten rules and codes of conduct that prescribe conduct in certain
          circumstances:
          A.   Mores
          B.   Folkways
          C.   Values
          D.   Norms

___ 8.   The routine social conventions of every day life are referred to as:
          A.   Norms
          B.   Values
          C.   Folkways
          D.   Mores

___ 9.   The norms that are considered to be central to the core functioning of society are:
          A.   Mores
          B.   Values
          C.   Norms
          D.   Folkways

___ 10.   A world view that the group values are superior to the individual's values is known
          as:
          A.   Anti-individualism
          B.   Communism
          C.   Collectivism
          D.   Socialism

___ 11.   This type of world view orientation values performance and success:
          A.   Goal orientation
          B.   Achievement orientation
          C.   Long-term orientation
          D.   Nurturing orientation

___ 12.   A _____ orientation values thrift and persistence in achieving goals.
          A.   global
          B.   long-term
          C.   mid-term
          D.   short-term

___ 13.   _____ allows a foreign organization to take charge of manufacturing and
          distributing a product in its country in return for a negotiated fee.
          A.   Franchising
          B.   A joint venture
          C.   Licensing

D.   An affiliated company

____ 14.   In the global general environment, managers must recognize the substantial differences that exist among countries':
                I.   Political systems
                II.   Economic systems
                III.   Legal systems
                IV.   Socio-cultural systems
        A.   I, II, and III
        B.   II, III, and IV
        C.   I, III, and IV
        D.   I, II, III, and IV

____ 15.   Which are the main impediments to an open global environment?
                I.   Governmental
                II.   Societal
                III.   Self-imposed
        A.   I and II
        B.   II and III
        C.   I and III
        D.   I, II, and III

Essay Questions

1.   What are the main impediments to an open global environment for trade?

2.   What are the forces that give rise to opportunities and threats in the global task environment?

3.   List the main forces that affect the global general environment.

4.   From the highest to the lowest level of foreign involvement, name the ways of expanding internationally.

Chapter 3: The Organizational Environment
and
Chapter 4: The Global Environment
featuring TREK Bike

Today more than ever, American businesses are feeling the heat from foreign competition. The combination of high tariffs at home, and cheaper labor costs in other countries, has made it increasingly difficult for American companies to be the foreign competition's prices. The competition is fierce, but American businesses can meet the challenges both at home and abroad by emphasizing the quality of American products and services. And the key to developing a successful quality strategy is management. Managers must include quality in every aspect of their business. This requires a huge shift in most managing styles. But it's got to be done. If quality is not made a top priority in American businesses, you can bet the foreign competition will leave them in the dust.

One company that knows the realities of the global market is Trek. Trek was founded in 1976 by a small group of biking enthusiasts who wanted to combine American manufacturing technology with precision hand craftsmanship to build the highest quality bicycles in the world. At first, everything ran smoothly. But by the mid-80s, Trek began to run into trouble. Joyce Keehn, Sales Manager of International Accounts, said, "In the 80s, we sort hit a brick wall, so to speak, in that we had high inventory, sales were down, we didn't have as many dealers as we should have had so we were sitting here with a lot of inventory and we were nearly bankrupt. And we had to relook at the situation while we were still running the business from a management standpoint as well as quality and getting our orders in and how we were dealing with the marketplace."

Trek had to develop a new game plan. The company decided to capitalize on its reputation as a leader in technology and quality craftsmanship. Keehn said, "When we look at our quality back in the 80s it wasn't what our U.S. dealers expected our quality to be, so we realized that if we wanted to increase our business domestically we had to increase our quality. And we began doing that for the U.S. market but an interesting thing that we found is that when we began to get into other markets like Germany and Japan their standards were much higher than what we were experiencing here in the states. So in effect these countries helped us increase our quality because we wanted to grow our business in these countries we listened to what the dealers and the market was expecting from us and we implemented those quality changes here."

Trek's international response was phenomenal and growth was rapid. Today, Trek sells its bicycles in 55 countries all over the world, with international sales accounting for 40 percent of its business. International competition strengthened Trek in domestic markets as well. As a result, Trek has grown 700 percent since 1988, making it the largest manufacturer of quality bicycles in the U.S. In fact, in 1992, when bicycle sales in the U.S. were down 6 percent, Trek's sales were up 17 percent. The key to Trek's amazing comeback was the increased emphasis on technology and quality in every aspect of the company. Richard A. Burke, Trek's president, said, "I think we see a lot of that in the interaction of the employees and our management. People who are on the firing line know how to do it better. And they are bringing that to management and saying "let's do it differently,' whether it can save a dollar in the production of a bike, or it can provide a higher level of customer service, I think it's people on the firing line that know what it takes, and management has to respond to that input."

Trek empowered its employees with decision making authority in several areas. It became a Trek policy that any employee can and should stop the assembly line if they detect the slightest problem with the product. Trek also organized employee group management teams. George B. Hausladen, quality assurance manager, said, "We've been using group management teams for about the last several years. The focus of those teams has been to try to plan our processes, and plan our work, and our products as early as possible into the cycle. And by doing this planning we are able to incorporate those ideas into the quality system."

Trek management also opened up communication, both internally and externally. Internally, every Trek employee knows the president's door is always open if they have questions or concerns. Externally, an open communication policy with employees, dealers, and customers affects Trek's design and marketing decisions. Dealer advice meetings allow dealers the opportunity to provide feedback, and see the results of previous suggestions. Field quality audits are set up to field questions from Trek's sales representatives. Harry Spehar, product manager, said, "One of the most important goals that I have in my job is to listen to what people are saying. I have to listen to what people internally are saying, or what the dealers are saying, or what my direct face-to-face interface has been with enthusiasts out in the field. Inside the Trek organization there's a lot of enthusiasts who love to ride, and we want to see that same impression come from the people that we're devising this product for."

Trek also realized that producing the highest quality bicycle in the world would require more than a shift in management function. The manufacturing process itself would have to be completely re-geared toward quality. At Trek this meant using the most innovative materials and technology available. Brad Wagner, engineer manager, said, "It's manufacturing's job to make sure that the product team's design is buildable. We have 10 of these manufacturing engineers. These guys design the fixtures and the processes. That's how each Trek gets the attention to detail, the flawless welds, and the detailed inspection that result in a great riding bike."

Trek engineers have become pioneers in the field of bicycle technology. They revolutionized the process in which bike frames are built, using stronger and lighter carbon fiber frames. Their most recent development is the carbon composite lug, which is used in the joints of the bicycle frame for increased, lightweight strength. Trek has also borrowed plasma-welding techniques used in the aerospace industry to create a higher quality bike.

In order to discover and correct problems before they occur, Trek conducts extensive testing on every model. In fact, every single frame is inspected to ensure quality standards before it is allowed out of the factory. One such test is called the high fatigue test, which was developed using a Japanese industrial standard. In the test, weights are placed on a bike frame to simulate the weight of the rider. The frame is then put through a rigorous set of tests to check its durability.

Dan Otis, test engineer, said, "Just about everyone I meet, when I tell them that I break bikes, is the easiest way to explain my job, and they say, wow that's really neat. But its not just that I break bikes. I go back and I measure how it was broken, how much force it takes, what kind of deflection occurred during this loading. And then I go back and look at the failure, and how it failed and why did it fail, and can we make it better? Can we make one part a little stronger, or a little weaker, so that the whole part is the same strength?"

Burke said, "If a customer is taken care of, they become a positive customer that says gee, Trek took care of me and I'm going to buy another Trek. And they are just as important and just as positive as the customer who gets a Trek and it works from the day they ride it out of the bicycle store."

Trek learned the hard way that even if your business is riding high you must address foreign competition to survive. Higher labor costs and expensive tariffs make it hard for most American businesses to compete on a price basis with foreign competition. A good way to be competitive is to develop high quality products and services. Trek restructured its management and employee relationships making quality an essential part of every aspect of the business. Trek also restructured its manufacturing process, resulting in the development of the most innovative materials and technology in the bicycle industry. Trek implemented inspections and extensive testing, with the emphasis on finding and correcting problems before they occur.

Trek's emphasis on quality as a competitive strategy for success in the global market has not only helped it to survive but prosper. President Burke said, "Particularly in the global marketplace where we are at a price disadvantage due to just the normal barriers. It is going to make quality the biggest differentiation in the competitive market that we face on the global scene. So quality is certainly number one domestically, but its is ultimately the most important standard internationally." They are proof positive that quality must be integrated into every management process for American businesses to survive in a global market.

Critical Thinking Questions

1.   Why was Trek unable to compete with foreign bicycle manufacturing based on price?

2.   Trek employees can stop the assembly line if they spot a defect. What are the advantages and disadvantages of this policy?

3.   What is the importance of Trek's "dealer advice meetings?"

Journal Entries
Chapter 5 - Ethics, Social Responsibility and Diversity

Entry 7:
1. Who are your stakeholders? How do they impact your decisions?
2. What factors impact your ethical (or unethical) behavior?
3. Which view of ethical behavior do you agree with most? Why?
4. Which ethical view do you tend to use in decision making?
5. What recent ethical dilemma have you faced? How did you decide what to do?
6. Use a recent example of an ethical dilemma discussed or encounter in the media (i.e., news, t.v. show, book) to analyze the factors that influence ethical decisions.

Entry 8:
1. How does workforce diversity affect you?
2. Is it more important for the classroom to use procedural or distributive justice? Why?
3. Is diversity considered important to your university or to a company you work(ed) for? Why or why not?
4. Have you ever fallen victim to one of the multicultural issues? Explain.

Chapter 5

Ethics, Social Responsibility, and Diversity

Chapter Outline

I.   Ethical Stances and Johnson & Johnson and Dow Corning

II.   Ethics and Stakeholders
    A.   Organizational Stakeholders
        1.   Shareholders
        2.   Managers
        3.   Non-managerial employees
        4.   Customers
        5.   Suppliers
        6.   Local and national community
    B.   Ethics Models
        1.   Utilitarian
        2.   Moral rights
        3.   Justice
    C.   Ethics In Action - The Use of Animals in Cosmetics Testing
    D.   Sources of an Organization's Code of Ethics
        1.   Societal Ethics
            a.   Ethics In Action - How Not to do Business in Argentina
        2.   Professional ethics
        3.   Individual ethics
    E.   What Behaviors are Ethical
    F.   Ethics In Action - Is It Right to Use Child Labor
    G.   Why Would Managers Behave Unethically Toward Other Stakeholders
    H.   Why Should Managers Behave Ethically

III.   Social Responsibility
    A.   Approaches to Social Responsibility
        1.   Obstructionist approach
        2.   Defensive approach
        3.   Accommodative approach
        4.   Pro-active approach
    B.   Why Be Socially Responsible
        1.   Social audit
        2.   Application of ethical standards and values
    C.   Promoting Ethics and Social Responsibility
        1.   Establishing ethical control systems
        2.   Developing an ethical culture

IV.   Managing an increasingly Diverse Workforce
    A.   The Ethical Imperative to Manage Diversity Effectively
        1.   Distributive Justice
        2.   Procedural Justice
    B.   Focus on Diversity - Age Discrimination at Schering Plough
    C.   Effectively Managing Diversity Makes Good Business Sense
    D.   Why Are Diverse Employees Sometimes Treated Unfairly
        1.   Biases
        2.   Stereotypes
        3.   Overt discrimination

V.   How to Manage Diversity Effectively
    A.   Increasing Diversity Awareness
    B.   Increasing Diversity Skills
        1.   Understanding how cultural differences affect working styles
        2.   Being able to communicate effectively with diverse people
        3.   Being flexible
    C.   Techniques for Increasing Diversity
    D.   The Importance of Top-Management Commitment to Diversity

VI.   Sexual Harassment
    A.   Forms of Sexual Harassment
        1.   Quid Pro Quo
        2.   Hostile work environment
    B.   Steps Managers Can Take to Eradicate Sexual Harassment
        1.   Develop and clearly communicate a sexual harassment policy endorsed by top management
        2.   Use a fair complaint procedure
        3.   Take a corrective action quickly
        4.   Provide education and training to organizational members
    C.   Ethics In Action - Finally a Corporate Tip Sheet on Sexual Harassment

Study Questions

True - False Questions

___ 1.   Ethics are moral principles about what is right and wrong.

___ 2.   The esteem that individuals or organizations gain from behaving ethically is known as folkways.

___ 3.   The defensive approach disregards social responsibility and will allow for engaging in illegal and unethical behavior.

____ 4.   The accommodative approach provides a willingness to do more than the law
            requires if asked to do so.

____ 5.   A social audit is a specific type of audit conducted by C.P.A.s who are Certified
            Fraud Examiners.

____ 6.   The ethics liaison monitors an organization's practices and procedures for ethics
            violations.

____ 7.   Distributive justice desires organizational resources to be disbursed based on
            personal characteristics the employees possess.

____ 8.   A bias is a simplistic and frequently wrong belief about characteristics of groups of
            people.

____ 9.   Using profanity in front of a highly sensitive employee would be quid pro quo
            sexual harassment.

____ 10.   A hostile work environment exists when the work place is "poisoned" by the
            conduct of an employee making the victim of the harassment less productive
            because of the harassment.

Multiple Choice Questions

____ 1.   Which of the following is **not** usually an organizational stakeholder?
            A.   Customers
            B.   Suppliers
            C.   Employees
            D.   Government

____ 2.   A decision that a manager would prefer to hide from stakeholders is a(n):
            A.   ethical decision.
            B.   situational decision.
            C.   unethical decision.
            D.   societal decision.

____ 3.   One item that accountants are governed by is known as _____ ethics.
            A.   societal
            B.   professional
            C.   reputational
            D.   ordinal

____ 4.   A manager's social responsibility is to make decisions that promote the welfare
            and well-being of:
                        I.   Society

II.   Government
III.   Stakeholders

    A.   I and III
    B.   I and II
    C.   II and III
    D.   I, II, and III

___ 5.   The _____ approach disregards social responsibility.
    A.   obstructionist
    B.   defensive
    C.   accommodative
    D.   pro-active

___ 6.   This approach demonstrates a willingness to only what the law requires and no more than that:
    A.   Obstructionist
    B.   Pro-active
    C.   Defensive
    D.   Accommodative

___ 7.   Practitioners of this approach will do more than the law requires if asked to do so:
    A.   Obstructionist
    B.   Accommodative
    C.   Defensive
    D.   Pro-active

___ 8.   The ____ approach has the strongest commitment to social responsibility.
    A.   obstructionist
    B.   accommodative
    C.   defensive
    D.   pro-active

___ 9.   An ethics officer who monitors an organization's practices and procedures for ethics violations is known as an ethics:
    A.   ombudsman.
    B.   liaison.
    C.   enforcer.
    D.   vice president.

___ 10.   Diversity differences are such characteristics as:
           I.   Age
           II.   Religion
           III.   Disabilities
           IV.   Socio-economic background
    A.   I, II, III, IV

B.   I, III, IV
C.   I, II, III
D.   II, III, IV

____ 11.   The moral principle calling for the disbursement of organizational resources to individuals based on positive contributions made to the organization is referred to as _____ justice.
A.   procedural
B.   distributive
C.   appraisal
D.   administrative

____ 12.   _____ is the systematic tendency to utilize information to help create inaccurate perceptions about other people.
A.   A stereotype
B.   A caricature
C.   Bias
D.   A psychographic evaluation

____ 13.   Which is **not** potentially a quid pro quo situation:
A.   Asking a fellow employee for a date.
B.   Offering sex for a promotion.
C.   Requesting sexual favors for a salary increase.
D.   Demanding sex for hiring an applicant.

____ 14.   A hostile work environment could be created by repetitive acts of which of these:
A.   Telling dirty jokes
B.   Profanity
C.   Remarks about a person's sexual prowess
D.   All of the above

____ 15.   The effective management of diversity can be accomplished if top management is committed to principles of:
            I.   Free-market systems
            II.   Distributive justice
            III.   Organizational diversity
            IV.   Procedural justice
A.   I, II, III, IV
B.   II, III, IV
C.   II and IV only
D.   I, II, III

Essay Questions

1. What are the sources of an organization's code of ethics?

2. Describe some forms of behavior of a socially responsible manager?

3. What are the approaches to social responsibility from the lowest to the highest approach?

4. What are the major sources of diversity in the workforce?

Chapter 5
Ethics, Social Responsibility, and Diversity

THE HIGH BID DILEMMA

A purchasing agent (PA) and his assistant are reviewing bids from seven companies to determine which company should receive a contract for bronze facing a clutch. The PA's assistant proposes that the bid should be awarded to Metaltech, the low bidder, which is located some 300 miles away. His boss, the PA agent, leans toward Spin Cast Systems, a nearby company, which has submitted a much higher bid. Both companies submitting bids have the ability to provide a quality product complete with delivery and support capabilities.

The PA attempts to persuade his assistant that the contract award should be awarded to Spin Cast Systems despite its higher bid that will create a budgetary problem. He informs his assistant that he has used Spin Cast's services previously. Moreover, Greg Sommers, the president of Spin Cast, is his personal friend, his fraternity brother, and his sailing companion. The PA tells his assistant, "You take care of your suppliers and they'll take care of you." In fact, to show his assistant that Sommers is a "nice guy," the PA will ask Sommers to invite the assistant to a house party.

CRITICAL THINKING QUESTIONS

1.   Does the issue of a "conflict of interest" surface in this exercise? If so, how? If not, why not?

2.   Will the purchasing assistant compromise his own ethics if he allows his boss to award the bid to Spin Cast Systems even though such an award will create a budget overrun and does not follow company regulations.

3.   Does the purchasing agent's assistant have any possible options if his boss decides to award the bid to Spin Cast?

A VERY FRIENDLY FELLOW

Bill and Shelly are having a conversation in the hallway. Shelly feels a certain degree of discomfort because Bill is standing very close to her. Ginny, another worker, meets them in the hallway, and Bill begins talking about the good time he had at a night club. He tells Shelly and Ginny that they should meet him and his friends after work at the Steak and Cap. Although Shelly, upset by his invitation, tells him she is busy and cannot make it, Ginny sees his invitation as a friendly social gesture from a co-worker.

When Shelly tells Ginny that she has to talk with her about a work project Bill decides to return to his office. Shelly informs Ginny that Bill will not leave her alone. She believes that he has been making sexual advances toward her and that she will be unable to work with him. Th problem is that he cannot seem to keep his hands off of her. He "touches" her by massaging her neck or by squeezing her arm even though she has repeatedly told Bill to stop.

CRITICAL THINKING QUESTIONS

1. What should Shelly do when she meets Bill at work?

2. What impact will Bill's "advances" have on their ability to work together on a new project?

3. Does Shelly have responsibility to report Bill's action to the personnel office?

COMPENSATION ISSUE

After Brenda, an African-American woman, and Sandy, a white woman, exchange pleasantries early on Friday morning, Brenda reveals to Sandy that she has just learned that another employee, June, who works in bookkeeping, receives $.30 an hour more pay. Brenda is upset by this information because both she and June began their employment with the company at the same time and they both perform similar functions.

Brenda believes that the company has "discriminated" against her because she is an African-American woman. She tells Sandy that she will hire an attorney to sue the company. Sandy suggests that the difference in pay, even for performing the same job function, may be a result of other considerations. For example, even though both women were hired at the same time, June may have had previous experience that allows the company to pay her a slightly higher salary. Brenda counters Sandy's argument by saying that a similar job within the same company should mean that each employee receives the same salary.

CRITICAL THINKING QUESTIONS

1. Is it ethical for employees to compare salaries when working for the same company? If so, why? If not, why not?

2. Do you believe that Brenda has been discriminated against by her company? If so, what type of discrimination?

3. Are there times when people working in the same company, hired at the same time, and doing the same work should be paid different salaries? Explain your answer.

COMPETITION OR REVENGE

A group of salespeople are discussing the impact a former employee is having on their current sales. Jack Rebeck, who was recently fired from this position, is now soliciting former clients. In one instance he has been successful in underbidding his old firm. The members of the sales group are concerned with Rebeck's competing for the same client pool.

Because Rebeck has limited financial resources, George, one member of the sales group, suggests that the company underbid Rebeck on projects. Jean, another former colleague, suggests that the group spread stories within the industry about the reasons Rebeck was terminated by the company, and finally, Jeff, the last member of the sales group, believes that bad-mouthing and undermining Rebeck is fruitless and will not have an impact on the company's business.

CRITICAL THINKING QUESTIONS

1. Is it ethical for an ex-employee to compete with a former company? If so, where? Under what circumstances?

2. Is it ethical for a company to attempt to undermine a former employee who is now a competitor?

3. If a company discusses the reason(s) an employee was terminated, does it violate employee confidentiality?

Journal Entries
Chapter 6 - The Manager as a Decision Maker

Entry 9:
1. What was a recent decision you had to make? How did you decide?
2. How did you pick your university or your major? Which approach did you seem to follow?

Entry 10:
1. Which decision making model did you follow in deciding your major?
2. Describe a decision you made recently with incomplete information. Why was the information incomplete? How did you decide?
3. Which Cognitive Biases do you have? How has it (have they) impacted your decisions?
4. Describe a recent group decision. Did you take advantage of the group or did the group cause a poor decision?
5. Is your university a learning organization? Would Senge define it as a learning organization?
6. Do you learn more from good decisions or bad ones?

Chapter 6

The Manager as a Decision Maker

Chapter Outline

I.   Calling Systems International

II. The Nature of Managerial Decision Making
    A.   Programmed Decision making
    B.   Non-programed Decision Making
    C.   The Classical Model
    D.   The Administrative Model
        1.   Bounded rationality
        2.   Incomplete Information
        3.   Risk and uncertainty
        4.   Ambiguous information
        5.   Time constraints and information costs
        6.   Satisficing
    E.   Management Insight - marketing Beavis and Butt-Head Trading Cards

III. Steps in the Decision Making Process
    A.   Recognize the Need for a Decision
    B.   Generate Alternatives
    C.   Assess Alternatives
        1.   Legality ethicalness
        2.   Economic feasibility
        3.   Practicality
    D.   Choose Among the Alternatives
    E.   Implement the Chosen Alternative
    F.   Learn From Feedback
    G.   Management Insight - British Petroleum's Decision Auditing Unit

IV. Cognitive Biases and Decision Making
    A.   Prior Hypothesis Bias
    B.   Representative Bias
    C.   Illusion of Control
    D.   Escalating Commitment
    E.   Awareness of Bias

V.   Group Decision Making
    A.   The Perils of Groupthink
    B.   Devil's Advocacy and Dialectical Inquiry

    C.   Diversity Among Decision Makers

    D.   Focus on Diversity - Diverse Employees Improve Decision Making at Hoechst Celanese

VI.   Organizational Learning and Creativity

    A.   Creating a Learning Organization

        1.   Personal mastery

        2.   Complex mental models

        3.   Team learning

        4.   Shared vision

        5.   System thinking

    B.   Promoting Individual Creativity

    C.   Promoting Group Creativity

        1.   Brainstorming

        2.   Nominal Group Technique

        3.   Delphi Technique

    D.   Promoting Creativity at the Global Level

    E.   Managing Globally - Building Cross-Cultural Creativity

Study Questions

<u>True - False Questions</u>

___ 1.   Routine decision making following established rules is called programmed decision making.

___ 2.   Judgment is the ability to develop a sound opinion based on available information.

___ 3.   The optimum decision is the most appropriate in light of what managers believe to be the most desirable consequences for society.

___ 4.   There can be no risk if an event cannot happen.

___ 5.   Heuristics are rules of thumb that simplify decision making.

___ 6.   Escalating commitment is a source of cognitive bias from continuing to fund a project when data illustrates the project is failing.

___ 7.   Critical analysis between two preferred alternatives is referred to as devil's advocacy.

___ 8.   Project blocking is a loss in productivity in brainstorming due to the unstructured nature of it.

___ 9.   Nominal group technique occurs when group members respond in writing to

51

questions posed by the group leader.

_____ 10.   A situation when group members read their suggestions to the whole group and then discuss and rank the alternatives is called the Delphi technique.

Multiple Choice Questions

_____ 1.   Which would **not** be a programmed decision:
   A.   Buying paper for the organization.
   B.   Defending the organization against a hostile take-over bid.
   C.   Choosing another travel agency for the organization.
   D.   Updating the organization's policy manual.

_____ 2.   March and Simon argue all of the following about managers, except:
   A.   They are boundedly rational.
   B.   They usually have access to all the information.
   C.   They rely on their intuition to make decisions.
   D.   They rely on their judgment to make decisions.

_____ 3.   Which of these is a step in the decision making process:
                     I.   Assessing alternatives
                     II.   Learning from feedback
                     III.   Implementing an alternative
   A.   I, II, III
   B.   I and III
   C.   II and III
   D.   I and II

_____ 4.   Cognitive biases are caused by systematic errors; sources of these errors include all but which of these:
   A.   Prior hypotheses
   B.   Representativeness
   C.   Duty of control
   D.   Escalating commitment

_____ 5.   When afflicted decision makers collectively embark on a dubious course of action without questioning the assumptions that underlie their decision, it is known as:
   A.   Groupthought
   B.   Groupthink
   C.   Clusterthink
   D.   Clusterthought

_____ 6.   Managers must take steps to promote organizational learning and creativity at the _____ level(s) to improve the quality of decision making.
   A.   individual and group

B.   individual

C.   group

D.   organizational and societal

___ 7.   _____ decision making occurs in response to unpredictable opportunities.

      A.   Programmed

      B.   Non-programmed

      C.   Classical

      D.   None of these

___ 8.   The ability to make sound decisions based on past experiences about the information available is called:

      A.   judgment.

      B.   heuristics.

      C.   intuition.

      D.   ethics.

___ 9.   The _____ model is an approach to decision making that explains why it is inherently uncertain and risky, and why managers usually make satisfactory rather than optimum decisions.

      A.   action-item

      B.   appraisal

      C.   assessment

      D.   administrative

___ 10.   Errors that people make over and over that result in poor decision making are:

      A.   systematic errors.

      B.   prior hypothesis bias.

      C.   representative bias.

      D.   heuristic errors.

___ 11.   A _____ bias is a cognitive bias resulting from the tendency to generalize inappropriately from a small sample.

      A.   prior hypothesis

      B.   representative

      C.   sampled

      D.   generalization

___ 12.   A critical analysis of two preferred alternatives in order to find an even better alternative for the organization to adopt is referred to as:

      A.   devil's advocacy.

      B.   dialectical inquiry.

      C.   cluster effect.

      D.   primary commitment.

____ 13.   This is an organization in which managers try to maximize the ability of individuals and groups to think creatively:
           A.   learned organization.
           B.   learning organization
           C.   organizational learning institution.
           D.   institutionalized learning.

____ 14.   The _____ technique is a decision making technique in which group members read their suggestions to the whole group and then discuss and rank the alternatives.
           A.   Delphi
           B.   production blocking
           C.   controlled illusion
           D.   nominal group

____ 15.   The technique in which group members respond in writing to questions posed by the group leader is known as the _____ technique.
           A.   Delta
           B.   Beta
           C.   Delphi
           D.   Alpha

Essay Questions

1.   The classical model of decision making includes what steps?

2.   Why is information incomplete?

3.   What are the six steps in decision making?

4.   What are Senge's principles for creating a learning organization?

Chapter 6
The Manager as a Decision Maker

In a global economy, sound business decisions require consideration of a number of important factors that may potentially affect a company's ability to meet its goals. The quality of managerial decisions can determine a company's success or failure. A recent study concluded that managers spend approximately 50 percent of their time dealing with the consequences of bad decision making.

It's important to understand decision making as it occurs in the business world. In this video, case study examples of two successful businesses—the Second City Theater in Chicago, Illinois, and Heavenly Ski Resort in Lake Tahoe, Nevada—explore the following decision making topics:

1. Managers make different decisions under different business conditions;
2. When managers take steps to explore and evaluate alternatives it leads to mom effective decisions; and
3. All managers need to be aware of the many factors that can affect the decision making process.

Broadly defined, decision making is a process of choosing among alternative courses of action. In the business world, this process takes place under varying conditions of certainty and risk. Decision making is more likely to be effective when approached in a series of steps that explore and evaluate alternatives.

1. Identify the problem;
2. Generate alternative solutions;
3. Evaluate the alternatives;
4. Select the best alternative;
5. Implement the decision; and
6. Evaluate the decision.

In order to evaluate a decision, managers must gather information that can shed light on its effectiveness. Although most managers would prefer to follow all of these decision making steps, time and circumstances don't always allow it. This decision making process can also be influenced by other important factors such as intuition, emotion and stress, confidence, and risk propensity.

Although Second City and Heavenly Lake Tahoe are very different businesses, they are both examples of companies that have made successful decisions under conditions of risk and uncertainty. Second City has grown from its roots as a small "mom and pop" theater, to a large, internationally known corporate enterprise. Rather than investing all its resources into its immensely popular old-town Chicago improv theater, the Second City has decided to translate its expertise into other ventures, such as television, corporate training, and other theaters in Toronto, suburban Chicago, and Detroit.

Joe Keefe, producer of Second City communications, said, "So much of what we do is in having people approach the decision making process from a group point of view, and allowing for input. It's difficult many times to find the time to listen to everyone but, I literally try to book out time weekly to meet with people. I meet with the directors after every project. I know what the heck happened: What do they think? How do they feel? What does the client feel? By the time you have all that information the decision is usually self evident. It's a matter of making certain that you get accurate information immediately, your client response issues are done immediately and then your intuition will tell you what's the right thing to do. Ninety-nine percent of my decisions are self evident once you have the right information."

Heavenly Lake Tahoe accommodates nearly 750,000 skiers per year, and competes as one of eight large Tahoe-area resorts. Like the Second City Theater, managers at Heavenly must make decisions affecting the growth of the company in less than ideal conditions. Malcolm Tibbets, vice president of mountain operations, said, "Quick decisions happen every hour of the day. Looking at the level of business coming into the base areas and making a quick decision to open an additional lift that was not otherwise scheduled or vice versa shutting down a lift in order to save some cost because the level of business is not going to warrant the operation of that lift. Whether to start the snow plows at midnight or wait until 3:00 in the morning. These kinds of decisions are continuous. You have to have people in positions that are unafraid to make those decisions without calling six people and wasting time collecting all the data. That's just part of the way this business works."

Although following the six decision-making steps may lead to a sounder decision making process, theory doesn't always play out in practice. Management may follow some steps, but perhaps not all of them, depending on the factors affecting the decision making process. Most of the managers are encouraged to make a decision right away and don't hold on to the problem. It's such a fast pace that I want them to just go on to the next thing and not hold the problem back. I've empowered them to pretty much make their own decisions. They were hired to do a job so I let them do the job. If there's something wrong we can discuss that later, but business must go on," said Steve Jacobson, director of food and beverage at Heavenly.

Sometimes it's easier to follow the steps of the decision making model. Kelly Leonard, associate producer at Second City, said, "Our northwest theater in Rolling Meadows we had seriously considered moving to Oakbrook. These people wanted us to move in, they were going to pay to have us move in and we had the luxury of a great deal of time to decide if we should leave or not. We decided not to primarily because the risk wasn't worth it at that point We really had a chance to make our lists of pros and cons which is exactly what we did and we finally decided to say no."

Making people laugh takes a lot of hard work and courage, as well as creativity and insight Decisions about artistic design don't always fit the mold of the decision making model. Certain factors, such as intuition, emotion and stress, or confidence and risk propensity can affect the decision making process. Leonard said, "We did a show which was a parody of Our Town and it was at times brilliant and at times not. It got great reviews, it was very intricate in its knowledge of Our Town. However, it demanded a understanding of the play and of the Second City form to really get all the jokes. What we found is that though critics loved it and many of us loved it here, the audience didn't understand it. We tried an advertising campaign to support it, which to that time we had not advertised much and it didn't work and people wouldn't come. So we had to switch over the show."

Not all factors affecting the decision making process are negative. Some, such as intuition, can assist an experienced manager in making decisions under pressure. Both the Second City Theater and Heavenly Lake Tahoe face the challenge of providing entertainment to consumers. In their day-to-day operations, both companies experience the need to make decisions in varying conditions of certainty, uncertainty, and risk. Both companies follow the steps of the decision making model when feasible. Identifying a problem, generating alternatives, evaluating the alternatives, selecting the best alternative, implementing the decision, and evaluating the decision. Factors such as intuition, emotion and stress, and confidence or risk propensity can also have an impact on the decision making process. Awareness of the nature of decision making, its important steps and influential factors may help managers minimize the time they spend responding to the consequences of poor decision malting. This can enable managers to spend more time maximizing opportunities for growth.

CRITICAL THINKING QUESTIONS

1. Decision making is described in the video as a series of steps. Do you agree with the six steps as outlined in the video? What additional procedures might be added to the process?

2. There are situations where decision making requires input from many people, and times when decisions have to be made by an individual. Describe a situation that would require wide input and one where an individual should make a decision without outside input. How do these situations differ?

3. Managerial decision making is affected by something called "risk propensity." What does this term mean? How can managers improve their risk propensity?

Journal Entries
Chapter 7 - The Manager as a Planner and Strategist

Entry 11:
1. What is your "mission statement"? Strategic plans and operational plans?
1. Describe the five forces that affect you as a student.
2. What are your competitive advantages - how are you distinguished from others in your major searching for jobs.

Entry 12:
1. What is your strategy in entering the job market after graduation-low cost or differentiated?
2. What are your long-term and short-term goals? How do you implement them?
3. What are your standing plans? What single use plans are you currently engaged in?
4. What is an objective of your university and how has it been translated through from strategy, operationalized and institutionalized?

Chapter 7

The Manager as a Planner and Strategist

Chapter Outline

I.   Gerald Pencer Starts a Cola War

II.   The Planning Process
        A.   Levels of Planning
                1.   Business-level plan
                2.   Function-level plan
        B.   Who Plans
        C.   Time Horizon of Plans
        D.   Standing Plans and Single-Use Plans
        E.   Why Planning is Important
        F.   Scenario Planning
        G.   Management Insight - Scenario Planning at Shell

III.   Determining the Organization's Mission and Goals
        A.   Defining the Business
        B.   Management Insight - Defining the Business of Seattle City Light
        C.   Establishing Major Goals

IV.   Formulating Strategy
        A.   SWOT Analysis
        B.   Management Insight - James Unruh Transforms Unisys
        C.   The Five Forces Model
                1.   The level of rivalry among organization in an industry
                2.   The potential of entry into an industry
                3.   The power of suppliers
                4.   The power of customers
                5.   The threat of substitute products

V.   Formulating Corporate-Level Strategies
        A.   Concentration on a Single Business
        B.   Diversification
                1.   Related diversification
                2.   Unrelated diversification
        C.   International Expansion
        D.   Management Insight - Caterpillar's International Strategy
        E.   Vertical Integration
        F.   Managing Globally - McDonald's Vertically Integrates to Preserve Quality

VI. Formulating Business-Level Strategy
    A.   Low Cost Strategy
    B.   Differentiation Strategy
    C.   "Stuck in the Middle"
    D.   Focused Low-Cost and Focused Differentiation Strategies

VII. Formulating Function-Level Strategies
    A.   Goals
        1.   Attain superior efficiency
        2.   Attain superior quality
        3.   Attain superior innovation
        4.   Attain superior responsiveness

VIII. Planning and Implementing Strategy

Study Questions

<u>True - False Questions</u>

____ 1.   A specific declaration of an organization's purpose is called a mission statement.

____ 2.   Corporate-level plans are fixed, static plans.

____ 3.   The corporate-level plan indicates in which industries and national markets an organization intends to compete.

____ 4.   A function is a department in which people have the same skills or use the same resources to perform their jobs.

____ 5.   Functional managers are managers who supervise one or more divisions within an organization.

____ 6.   A time horizon is the infinite duration of a plan for an organization.

____ 7.   When an organization purchases a company to turn it around for a profit, it is known as an unrelated diversification.

____ 8.   Multidomestic strategy is the opposite of global strategy.

____ 9.   A focused low-cost strategy serves only one market segment and tries to be the lowest cost provider serving that segment.

____ 10.   A function-level strategy indicates how a function intends to achieve its goals and how it will add value.

Multiple Choice Questions

___ 1.   Which is **not** a step in the planning process?
    A.   Determining a mission and goals
    B.   Formulating strategy
    C.   Appraisal and assessment
    D.   Implementing strategy

___ 2.   A good plan does **not** do which of these:
    A.   Builds commitment for the goals
    B.   Gives direction and purpose
    C.   Eliminates the different functions and divisions of an organization
    D.   Makes managers accountable for their goals

___ 3.   Which is a false statement concerning a mission statement?
    A.   It is a specific declaration of the organization's purpose
    B.   It identifies the organizations's products
    C.   It identifies the organization's customers
    D.   It distinguishes the organization from its competitors

___ 4.   A division is a unit that:
    A.   has its own set of managers.
    B.   has its own functions or departments.
    C.   competes in s a distinct industry.
    D.   is all of these.

___ 5.   What level decides the organizational mission?
    A.   Division
    B.   Corporate
    C.   Functional
    D.   Departmental

___ 6.   Corporate-level strategy utilizes what time frame for planning?
    I.   Short-term
    II.   Intermediate-term
    III.   Long-term
    A.   II and III
    B.   I and III
    C.   III only
    D.   I and II

___ 7.   This is a plan that indicates haw a division intends to compete against its rivals in an industry:
    A.   Division-level strategy
    B.   Business-level strategy

C.   Corporate-level strategy
D.   Functional-level strategy

___ 8.   A _____-level plan are goals managers purpose to pursue to help the division
attain its business-level goals.
A.   functional
B.   divisional
C.   business
D.   corporate

___ 9.   This strategy utilizes short-term or intermediate-term planning, but not long-term
planning, to achieve its goals:
A.   Divisional-level
B.   Corporate-level
C.   Functional-level
D.   Business-level

___ 10.   Which time period is a correct representation?
                              I.   Short-term is 1 to 3 years
                              II.   Intermediate-term is 3 to 5 years
                              III. Long-term is 5 or more years
A.   I, II, and III
B.   I and II
C.   II and III
D.   III only

___ 11.   Scenario planning is also known as _____ planning.
A.   time
B.   contingency
C.   strategic
D.   diversification

___ 12.   Performance gains that result when individuals coordinate their action is called:
A.   Coordinated strategy
B.   Focused diversification
C.   Synergy
D.   Entropy

___ 13.   _____ integration is a strategy that allows an organization to create value by
producing its own inputs or distributing and selling its own outputs.
A.   Horizontal
B.   Vertical
C.   Linear
D.   Diagonal

_____ 14.   _____ strategy distinguishes an organization's products from its competitors products in areas such as quality and design.
  A.   Low-cost
  B.   Focused low-cost
  C.   Differentiation
  D.   Focused differentiation

_____ 15.   This strategy serves only one segment of the overall market and tries to be the most differentiated organization serving the segment:
  A.   Focused differentiation
  B.   Low-cost differentiation
  C.   Multidomestic
  D.   Focused global

Essay Questions

1.   What are the broad, main steps in planning?

2.   What is a SWOT analysis and why is it useful?

3.   What types of strategies are utilized at the corporate-level?

4.   Strategy implementation requires managers to do what five items?

Chapter 7
The Manager as a Planner and Strategist
And Chapter 19
The Management of Innovation,
Product Development, and Entrepreneurship

Mountain biking, one of the fastest growing sports in America both recreationally and competitively, is debuting in the 1996 summer Olympics. It's roots began to spread in the late 1970's. And as Mountain biking grew so did one of the premier companies in the cycling business: Specialized Bicycle Components. Specialized Bicycle is one the industry's rags riches stories. To appreciate the entrepreneurial spirit that started the company, and still guides it today, it's important to understand the company's goals, its position in the cycling industry, the unique characteristics of the business, Specialized Bicycle's approach to it, and the connection between foreign and domestic operations and the company's critical strategy for success.

Specialized Bicycle Components' headquarters is in Morganville, California at the southern tip of Silicon Valley. This area is a Mecca for both micro and mainframe computers, and for cycling. Today Specialized holds a 65% share of all mountain bikes sold with 6,000 retailers in 25 countries and approximately 200 employees in the U.S. Specialized Bicycle's founder and president Mike Sinyard was a young cyclist touring Europe in 1974 with about $700 in his pocket and a lot more free time when he fortuitously met some Italians. His passion and admiration for the Italian high-quality handle bars led him to invest his remaining dollars to become an importer on a shoestring. Back in America Sinyard's first company catalog was hand written. He tried working at other jobs to get working capital to import parts, but a friend finally convinced him that climbing to success meant getting capital from others. In this case, advance payment from dealers. Given Mike's credit history his other approach to raising capital was to get everything cash on delivery, or COD.

Dealers recognized the quality of Mike's parts and, in those days, communication in the cycling community was based largely on word of mouth. As one dealer put it, "Other suppliers could wait for payment, but with Mike if we didn't pay him we knew he wouldn't eat." Sinyard recalled those early days, "What I found in doing business really is that if you work with people, with being very genuine and very straight with people, then people will accept you."

Specialized Bicycle's first manufactured product was a tire. Designing a tire was the turning point in the business. The tire was lightweight, sturdy, and lasted a lot longer than any existing tire available to the consumer. This was the first implementation of Sinyard's philosophy of moving the innovation and quality of racing technology to the consumer. The tires were a success, in large part because Specialized focused on doing it right. Sinyard said, "We really kind of pointed out how important the tires are on the bike. This is the most important square inch of the bicycle and that's the square inch that's touching the ground."

Today Specialized is the top seller of cycling tires. In 1980 the company introduced it's first mountain bike, the Stump Jumper. At $750 it was an immediate success. Today it remains the company's flagship bike although the model line has expanded and the technology has produced lighter, faster, and safer bikes. After a visit to the far east in 1975 manufacturing was moved to Taiwan. Only Specialized Bicycle's top of the line model is still manufactured in the U.S.

Chris Murphy, director of marketing bikes explained the company's marketing strategy, "Customers don't buy the second or third or fourth best brand when they spend $600.00. Our bikes range from $269 to $5000. There's a certain threshold where people say: 'I'm not settling for second best. I'm into the sport. I know exactly what I want. I want these features and I want the best bike out there.' And so if you expect to compete in that image/perception price point, your cutting edge image is critical." Accessories are a major player in the company's success, including, tires, helmets, lights, water bottles, shoes, and clothing.

Research and testing at the Morganville headquarters also plays an important role. A key element of success at Specialized is innovation. Chris Murphy said, "We're involved in this sport. We ride, we go to the races, we're there with the racing teams. We hope we can identify the trends a little quicker and come back and say 'We need to take a look at this. We need to study this. And let's do more homework on this.' I think that what really has set us apart in the last 20 years is going out and finding something really fast and coming back and saying, 'Okay is this something?, Are we in? Ah, forget it,' and moving on to something else and deciding where we should go."

Recently Specialized has gotten involved in land access issues by hiring a full time coordinator to track public issues and legislative actions Linda DuPriest, advocacy coordinator, explained, "My role as advocacy coordinator is to deal with social issues that affect the bicycle business or social issues opportunities for the bike industry such as mountain bike trail advocacy and access issues, teaching responsible, ethical, back country use to mountain bikers. Communicating to mountain bike consumers and dealers about the importance of behaving yourself on a trail."It's a highly competitive marketplace. Specialized Bicycle's competitors include Trek, Cannondale, GE and a host of small customized manufacturers. Most of the competitors are also looking to both foreign and domestic collaborators. Gearing, shocks, handlebars, and stems and frames are some of the components provided by collaborators.

The company's philosophy or goads are clearly stated in the lobby on a stone plaque: Customer Satisfaction, Quality, Innovation, Teamwork, Profitability. Specialized Bicycle's healthy position in an industry faced with tight profit margins exerts pressure to continually find something that is lighter, faster, and sturdier. It's an industry where the players look for ways to expand the overall market. It's also an industry populated by a small network of innovators. Specialized is committed to expanding a market that's maturing and becoming crowded with competitors. The company is one that can't be separated from its president and founder, and his employees seem to be from the same mold. From Sinyard on down everyone has a passion for cycling.

Employees are the customers. Specialized Bicycle's strategy is Sinyard's strategy. Sinyard is very good at defining what it takes to create an environment for success. He has a vision for success, knows his limits, and seeks people with enthusiasm and passion. He said, "Part of the creative process is just trying new things and challenging people to do new things. And even if you do something that doesn't work you learn something from it and that's one of the things I really encourage people to do is take a risk and make it happen. Take a risk and if you make a mistake that's fine just learn from it and continue moving."

CRITICAL THINKING QUESTIONS

1. What does the narrator of this video mean when he says that Specialized is a company that can't be separated from its president and founder?

2. How crucial do you think Sinyard's "people skills" were to the start up of his company.

3. What strategies does Specialized pursue to stay abreast of trends in the cycling industry?

Journal Entries
Chapter 8 - Managing Organizational Structure

Entry 13:

1. How is your university or your employer designed and structured? Does it fit the organization's goals?
2. What is your family's organizational structure? How are the four fundamental elements exhibited? How is effective coordination achieved?
3. Describe the design of your "job" as a student in terms of the job characteristics model. How motivating is it?
4. Which job design strategy should be used for improving the job of "student?"
5. How does your employer/university coordinate the efforts of all its members (i.e., the faculty, staff, and students)?
6. Describe the chain of command of your family, university or work place. How does the chain impact decision-making?

Chapter 8

Managing Organizational Structure

Chapter Outline

I.   Kinko's Changes Its Organizational Structure

II.   Designing Organizational Structure
      A.   The Organizational Environment
      B.   Strategy
      C.   Technology
           1.   Small-batch technology
           2.   Mass-production technology
           3.   Continuous-process technology
      D.   Human Resources

III. Grouping Tasks Into Jobs: Job Design
      A.   Job Enlargement and Job Enrichment
      B.   The Job Characteristic Model
           1.   Skill/variety
           2.   Task identity
           3.   Task significance
           4.   Autonomy
           5.   Feedback

IV.   Grouping Jobs into Functions and Divisions
      A.   Functional Structure
      B.   Divisional Structures: Product, Geographic, and Market
      C.   Management Insight - Viacom's Product Structure
      D.   Management Insight - From Geographic to Market Structure at Eastman Kodak
      E.   Matrix Design
      F.   Product Team Structure
      G.   Management Insight - Product Teams Produce Competitive Advantage
      H.   Hybrid Structure

V.   Coordinating Functions and Divisions
      A.   Allocating Authority
           1.   Tall and flat organizations
           2.   The minimum chain of command
           3.   Centralization and decentralization of authority
      B.   Managing Globally - Proctor & Gamble's New World Hierarchy
      C.   Types of Integrating Mechanisms

1.   Direct contact
2.   Liaison roles
3.   Task forces
4.   Cross-functional teams
5.   Integrating roles
6.   Matrix structure

VI.   Strategic Alliances and Network Structure
    A.   Innovations in Organizational Architecture
    B.   Managing Globally - Nike's Network Structure

Study Questions

True - False Questions

___ 1.   Organizational design is a formal system of task and reporting relationships working together to achieve organizational goals.

___ 2.   The Ford Taurus is an example of small-batch technology.

___ 3.   Mass-production technology utilizes a formal organizational structure with little flexibility.

___ 4.   Job enlargement increases the number of different tasks in a job by changes in the division of labor.

___ 5.   Market structure is also known as custodial structure.

___ 6.   The matrix structure is an organizational structure that simultaneously groups people and resources by function and geography.

___ 7.   A product team structure is one in which employees are temporarily assigned to a cross-functional team and report only to the division manager.

___ 8.   Span of control is the number of subordinates who report directly to a manager.

___ 9.   A task force, or advisory committee, is composed of managers from various organizations who met to solve market problems.

___ 10.   Outsourcing uses other organizational departments to produce goods and services.

Multiple Choice Questions

_____ 1. Which is **not** one of the main determinants of organizational structure:
   A. Technology
   B. Human resources
   C. Strategy
   D. Internal environment

_____ 2. Which are structures that managers can utilize?
   I. Product
   II. Matrix
   III. Product team
   IV. Geographic
   A. I, II, IV
   B. II, III, IV
   C. I, II, III, IV
   D. II and IV

_____ 3. No matter which structure manager chooses, he or she must do:
   A. Decide how to distribute authority
   B. Decide how many levels of authority
   C. Decide the balance between centralization and decentralization
   D. All of these

_____ 4. Which is **not** an integrating mechanism?
   A. Liaison roles
   B. Task forces
   C. Cross-functional teams
   D. Market structure

_____ 5. A Rolls Royce is an example of _____ technology.
   A. small-batch
   B. mass-production
   C. continuous-process
   D. flexible-production

_____ 6. This type of technology is based on the use of automated machines that are programmed to perform the same operations repeatedly:
   A. Small-batch
   B. Mass-production
   C. Continuous-process
   D. Repetitive-production

_____ 7. Which is **not** an example of continuous-process technology:
   A. Oil refineries

B.   Micro-breweries
C.   Steel mills
D.   Nuclear power stations

_____ 8.   Job _____ increases the number of different tasks in a given job by changing the division of labor.
A.   enlargement
B.   enrichment
C.   simplification
D.   empowerment

_____ 9.   Increases in the degree of responsibility a worker has over his or her job is referred to as job:
A.   empowerment.
B.   enlargement.
C.   enrichment.
D.   entitlement.

_____ 10.   This organizational structure is composed of separate business units within which are the functions that work together to produce a specific product for a specific customer:
A.   Divisional
B.   Functional
C.   Product
D.   Market

_____ 11.   Customer structure is also referred to as a _____ structure.
A.   matrix
B.   market
C.   product
D.   managerial

_____ 12.   The _____ structure is an organizational structure that simultaneously groups people and resources by function and product.
A.   market
B.   geographic
C.   matrix
D.   product

_____ 13.   This is a group of managers from different departments brought together to perform organizational tasks:
A.   Hybrid team
B.   Synergistic team
C.   Product
D.   Cross-functional

_____ 14.   The _____ states an organization's chain of command which specifies the relative authority of each manager.
A.   totem pole of authority
B.   hierarchy of authority
C.   span of control
D.   matrix of control

_____ 15.   A network structure is created with whom?
                        I.   Distributors
                        II.   Manufacturers
                        III. Customers
                        IV.   Suppliers
A.   I, II, III, IV
B.   II, III, IV
C.   I, II, III
D.   I, II, IV

Essay Questions

1.   When does a strategic alliance become a network structure?

2.   What are the factors affecting organizational structure?

3.   List the job characteristics that lead to the Job Characteristics model's outcomes?

4.   From the most simple to the most complex, what are the types of integrating mechanisms?

Chapter 8
Managing Organizational Structure

In the past, a corporation was structured much like the military, with a formal chain of command and division of labor. Over time, may companies came to realize that the bureaucratic structure of the traditional corporation can often cause breakdowns in communication and lower efficiency.

Manufacturers of products in relatively unchanging environments often take a mechanistic approach to production. In such environments, employees strictly adhere to their job descriptions. However, companies that depend on their ability to continuously introduce new innovations usually take a more organic approach, giving employees more room to make decisions and communicate outside the chain of command. Some companies may choose to radically modify or reengineer their structure.

Big Apple Bagels and St. Louis Bread Company are two rapidly growing businesses that share a similar market. However, each organization is structured quite differently. Whatever the structure, for an organization to be successful, it must be responsive to its customers. This operating principle runs a lot deeper than just making sure the right kind of cheese gets put on a turkey sandwich.

Many companies are finding that changing the way in which they are organized improves their responsiveness. For example, they may choose to simplify their structure and reduce the layers of management, thus reducing the layers in the chain of command. Another option is to widen the spans of control. The traditional organization has a tall structure and a narrow span of control. This means managers have few subordinates who report directly to them. A company with a flat organizational structure has a wide span of control with fewer reporting levels.

Many companies are empowering their employees and allowing them to make decisions on their own rather than insisting that they report to various levels of management When Paul Stolzer opened the first Big Apple Bagel store in 1985, he had no idea that in the short span of seven years his small store would grow into a franchise that boasts 75 stores with more opening all the time. Stolzer said, "The stores have changed quite extensively over the years. We are actually a fourth or fifth generation store right now. Initially the stores were set up as strictly bagel bakeries with a predominant product being bagels and cream cheese. We've progressed to a more aggressive stature, adding a few more dimensions to our operation in that we have dine-in facilities, a more extensive sandwich menu, and a very, very strong coffee program. We're still progressing. That's one thing that never ends."

One thing that hasn't changed is Big Apple Bagels' open-door policy. From top management to line workers, communication channels are wide open. Jim Lentz, director of training for the company said, "At Big Apple Bagels we have an open door policy between the franchisee and the franchisor, and between the ultimate consumer and the franchisor in that we encourage people to come up with suggestions, new products, new

ideas. We're never further than a phone call or a stop away. We're continually in the franchisee's stores to make sure that their operation meets our specifications."
In 1987, Ken Rosenthal opened his first St Louis Bread Company store in Kirkwood, Missouri, with used baking equipment. Today, St. Louis Bread company operates over 50 stores in the St. Louis area, with stores opening in other Midwestern markets as well. The growth happened quickly, forcing the company to change its organizational structure. Originally, it was a small store with 17 employees. When it became a large chain, employing over 1,000 people, a more traditional organizational structure was needed.

When a company is growing, it may need to use some of the concepts of reengineering. Reengineering entails the radical redesign of business processes to achieve major gains in cost, service, or time. For example, by mid-1992, St. Louis Bread was growing at a frantic pace. The partners decided it was time to slow down and take a breath. They began to realize that the opportunistic approach wouldn't work anymore.

They had reached a point where the controls and information systems they had in place were inadequate for a larger operation. New equipment was purchased to automate processes on the line. Thirty thousand dollar point of purchase cash registers were installed to track everything from sales per hour to sales per stock keeping unit to sales by stores.

Doron Berger said, "The organization at St. Louis Bread Company is probably not atypical of many organizations. While we have a hierarchical structure in terms of someone is ultimately accountable for the results of the business. We do fight vigorously to maintain a flat organization. In other words, there aren't a lot of layers between the president CEO and the people who are on the front lines. I think we have succeeded because of the effort we have put into that."

In November of 1983, Au Bon Pain, the dominant bakery/cafe chain in the country acquired St. Louis Bread Company. Au Bon Pain's stores were all in urban areas. St. Louis Bread would enable them to tap into the suburban market. David Hutkin said, "Our organizational structure has not changed dramatically. It really hasn't changed since the acquisition. We've continued to run the company very independent of the parent company, and we're still building stores and expanding the concept As far as the organization, basically we're still doing the same things as we were doing before."

A company like Big Apple Bagels is considered to be a boundaryless organization. In such an organization, the corporate structure is more horizontal than vertical. Boundaryless businesses are typically organized around core customer oriented processes, such as communication, customer contact, and managing quality. In order to enjoy the benefits a horizontal organization offers, four boundaries must be overcome:

- Authority
- Task
- Political
- Identity

Even a relatively boundaryless company has an authority boundary. Some people lead, others follow. To overcome problems that may arise, managers must learn how to lead and still remain open to criticism. Their "subordinates" need to be trained and encouraged not only to follow but also to challenge their superiors if there is an issue worth considering. As one Big Apple executive said, "I think there are some natural boundaries that occur between a franchisor and a franchisee, or an employee and an employer. What we try to do at Big Apple Bagels is to eliminate those boundaries by keeping the phone line open at all times as well as the fact that a lot of us have been franchisees as well as now being a franchisor so we know what it's like to sit on both sides of the table and to be able to talk to the franchisee from the standpoint of we were there at one time as well and we have that empathy for their position."

The task boundary arises out of the "it's not my job" mentality. A task boundary can be overcome by clearly defining who does what when employees from different departments divide up work.

The political boundary derives from the differences in political agendas that often separate employees and can cause conflict. This is closely related to identity boundary. The identity boundary emerges due to an employee tendency to identify with those individuals or groups with whom they have shared experiences, or with whom they share fundamental values.

To overcome the identity boundary, employees and management need to be trained to gain an understanding of the business as a whole and avoid the "us versus them" mentality. A good way to do this is by forming cross functional teams, in which tasks are shared and cross training simply happens as a result of employee interaction.
The new boundaryless organization relies on self-managed work teams. It reduces internal boundaries that separate functions and create hierarchical levels. A horizontal corporation is structured around core, customer-oriented processes.

Lines of communication are very open, allowing line-level employees to communicate their questions and concerns directly to those at the management and executive level. Not all organizations are structured the same way. There are factors to consider such as organizational size, culture, and production volume. These factors may indicate that under some circumstances, a tall organizational structure may be more appropriate than a flat structure. Companies in the future may change or alter the way they operate but customer satisfaction, quality, and efficiency will always be the primary goals.

CRITICAL THINKING QUESTIONS

1.   If companies today are working so hard to break down boundaries, why is it that there are boundaries in the first place?

2.   What are some new technologies that will help managers keep lines of communi-cation open to employees? To customers?

3. The video mentions that St. Louis Bread Company had to use a more traditional organizational structure when it grew rapidly. Why do you think that was necessary? What do you think the company gains by adopting such a structure? What does it lose?

4. What new communication tools do you think lie on the horizon?

Journal Entries
Chapter 9 - Organizational Control and Culture

Entry 14:
1.   How well is your university controlling its efficiency, quality, responsiveness, and innovation?
2.   How is control exercised in your family or work place? Does it enhance or weaken your efficiency and effectiveness?
3.   What type of control systems do you use—for yourself? for group assignments? at work?
4.   How do you control your performance as a student? What measures do you use?
5.   How do you control your financial resources? Do you have a budget? What are your "key ratios" that measure your liquidity?
6.   What expense is the largest part of your budget? How could you more effectively manage that cost?
7.   How do you use goals and goal setting to control behavior?
8.   Describe your basic family or work place rules and how they impact the culture and ethics of the groups members.
9.   How were you socialized into your university? What kinds of rites and ceremonies are used?
10. What are the key stories and legends that make your campus unique?

Chapter 9

Organizational Control and Culture

Chapter Outline

I. Different Approaches to Output Control Create Different Cultures
    A. Giddings and Lewis
    B. Informix

II. Organizational Control
    A. Importance of Control
        1. Efficiency
        2. Quality
        3. Responsiveness
        4. Innovation
    B. Control Systems
        1. Feedforward control
        2. Concurrent control
        3. Feedback control
    C. The Control Process
        1. Establish standards of performance
        2. Measure actual performance
        3. Compare actual performance to standards
        4. Evaluate comparison and take corrective action

III. Output Control
    A. Financial Measures of Performance
        1. Profit ratios
        2. Liquidity ratios
        3. Leverage ratios
        4. Activity ratios
    B. Organizational Goals
    C. Operating Budgets
    D. Managing Globally - Japan's New Concern for Output Control
    E. Problems with Output Control
    F. Ethics In Action - Trouble at Sears

IV. Behavior Control
    A. Direct Supervision
    B. Management by Objective
        1. Specific goals and objectives established at each level of the organization
        2. Managers and subordinates together determine the subordinates' goals

3. Managers and subordinates periodically review the subordinates' progress towards meeting goals
   C. Bureaucratic Control
   D. Management Insight - Never Underestimate the Power of Rules
   E. Problems with Bureaucratic Control

V. Organizational Culture and Clan Control
   A. Values and Norms: Creating a Strong Organizational Culture
      1. Values of the Founder
      2. Socialization
      3. Ceremonies and Rites
         a. Rites of passage
         b. Rites of integration
         c. Rites of enhancement
      4. Stories and language
   B. Management Insight - Ray Kroc: McDonald's Hero
   C. Culture and Managerial Action
      1. Planning
      2. Organizing
      3. Leading
      4. Controlling

Study Questions

True - False Questions

_____ 1. Control systems are informal monitoring and evaluation systems that provide managers with information about how well the organization's strategy and structure are working.

_____ 2. Feedforward and feedback controls are, in essence, the same thing.

_____ 3. Concurrent control gives managers immediate feedback on the efficiency of inputs being transformed to outputs.

_____ 4. Feedback control allows managers to anticipate problems before they arise.

_____ 5. Management by objectives is a goal-setting process in which a manager controls behavior by means of a comprehensive system of rules and procedures.

_____ 6. Bureaucratic control is the negotiation of specific goals and objectives for the subordinate to achieve and on which to be evaluated.

_____ 7. Organizational culture is the control exerted on individuals and groups in an

81

organization by shared norms, values, and expectations.

_____ 8. Clan control is the set of values and norms that control the ways in which individuals and groups in an organization interact with each other and achieve organizational goals.

_____ 9. Organizational initiation is the process by which newcomers learn an organization's values and norms to perform effectively.

_____ 10. The three types of rites are the rites of passage, integration, and enhancement.

Multiple Choice Questions

_____ 1. Which are types of organizational rites:

I.	Enrichment
II.	Enhancement
III.	Integration
IV.	Passage
V.	Socialization

  A. II, III, IV
  B. I, III, IV, V
  C. II, IV, V
  D. I, III, V

_____ 2. The purpose of this rite is to learn and internalize norms and values:
  A. Rite of integration
  B. Rite of passage
  C. Rite of socialization
  D. Rite of enrichment

_____ 3. An office Christmas party is an example of a rite of:
  A. Passage
  B. Enhancement
  C. Enrichment
  D. Integration

_____ 4. Motivating commitment to norms and values is part of the rite of:
  A. Enhancement
  B. Integration
  C. Enrichment
  D. Socialization

_____ 5. To calculate the return on investment, _____ profits before taxes divided by _____.
  A. gross; total assets

B.   net; net assets
C.   net; total assets
D.   gross; net assets

___ 6.   The current ration is considered a _____ ratio.
A.   profit
B.   liquidity
C.   leverage
D.   activity

___ 7.   The quick ratio is computed by dividing current assets - inventory by:
A.   current liabilities.
B.   total liabilities.
C.   total assets.
D.   sales revenues.

___ 8.   The _____ ratio measures how far profits can decline before managers cannot
meet interest charges; if the ratio is less than __, the organization is technically
insolvent.
A.   debt-to-assets; 0
B.   quick; 1
C.   times-covered; 1
D.   times-covered; 0

___ 9.   Managers perform all but which of these as part of their main functions:
A.   Leading
B.   Organizing
C.   Programming
D.   Controlling

___ 10.   Controlling is a four-step process; which is **not** one of the steps?
A.   Establishing performance standards
B.   Measuring competitor's performance
C.   Comparing actual performance against performance standards
D.   Evaluating the results and taking corrective action

___ 11.   The main mechanisms that managers use to monitor output are:
            I.   Organizational goals
            II.   Financial measures of performance
            III.   Operating budgets
            IV.   Employee surveys
A.   I and II
B.   II, III, and IV
C.   I, II, and III
D.   I, II, III, and IV

_____ 12.   To shape behavior and induce employees to work toward organizational goals, managers utilize:
    A.   direct supervision.
    B.   management by objective
    C.   bureaucratic control
    D.   all of these.

_____ 13.   Clan control is:
    A.   the control exerted on individuals and groups by shared norms, expectations, and values.
    B.   illegal.
    C.   part of behavioral control.
    D.   part of output control.

_____ 14.   In an _____ culture, managers are likely to lead by example.
    A.   conservative
    B.   clan
    C.   innovative
    D.   imperial

_____ 15.   In a _____ culture, a management by objective system and constant monitoring of progress will be utilized.
    A.   clan
    B.   conservative
    C.   innovative
    D.   imperial

Essay Questions

1.   What are the types of control, and in which stages are they utilized?

2.   What are the four steps in organizational control?

3.   Describe three mechanisms of control for output control.

4.   Name the factors that create a strong organizational culture.

Chapter 9

Organizational Control and Culture

For some organizations, the slogan "focus on customers" is merely a slogan. At Southwest Airlines, however, it is a daily goal. For example, Southwest employees responded quickly to a customer complaint: Five students who commuted weekly to an out-of-state medical school notified Southwest that the most convenient flight got them to class 15 minutes late. To accommodate the student, Southwest moved the departure time up by a quarter of an hour.

Southwest Airlines is an organization that has built its business and corporate culture around the tenets of total quality management. Focus on the customer, employee involvement and empowerment, and continuous improvement are not just buzzwords to Southwest employees or to Herb Kelleher, CEO of Southwest Airlines in Dallas. In fact, Kelleher has even enlisted passengers in the effort to strengthen the customer-driven culture. Frequent fliers are asked to assist personnel manager in interviewing and selecting prospective flight attendants. Focus groups are used to help measure passenger response to new services and to help generate new ideas for improving current services. Additionally, the roughly 1,000 customers who write to the company every week generally get a personal response within four weeks. It's no surprise that in 1994, for the third consecutive year, southwest won the U.S. Department of Transportation's Triple Crown Award for best on-time performance, best baggage handling, and fewest customer complaints.

THE AIRLINE INDUSTRY

Southwest has been posting hefty profits in an industry that lost $4 billion between 1990 and 1993. Since the 1978 Airline Deregulation Act, constant fare wars and intense competition have contributed to a turbulent environment for the industry. Under deregulation, the government no longer dictates where a given airline will fly and which cities should have service. Rates and service are now determined through competitive forces. The impact on the industry has been tremendous. In 1991 alone, three carriers went through bankruptcy and liquidation, and in early 1992, TWA sought protection from its creditors. Very few airlines, such as Southwest, American, and Delta, have continued to grow into the 1990s.

In 1994, when industry earnings were only $100 million (on revenues of $54 billion), Southwest earned $179 million while spending an industry-low 7 cents a mile in operating costs. The following year, despite facing new competition from upstart low-cost airlines, Southwest had record earnings of nearly $183 million.

Both external factors, such as the price of jet fuel and the strength of the economy, and internal factors, including routing system designs, computerized reservation systems, and motivated, competent employees, help to determine success. The airline industry is capital intensive, with large expenditures for planes. In addition, carriers must provide superior customer service. Delayed flights, lost baggage, overbooked flights,

85

cancellations, and unhelpful airline employees can quickly alienate an airline's passengers.

SOUTHWEST'S CORPORATE STRATEGY

Herb Kelleher has been the primary force in developing and maintaining a vision and strategy which have enabled Southwest Airlines to grow and maintain profitability. Created in the late 1960s as a low-fare, high-frequency, short-haul, point-to-point, singe-class, noninterlining, fun-loving airline, it expands by "doing the same old thing at each new airport," Kelleher reports.

"Taking a different approach" is the Southwest way, which has allowed the airline to maintain a 15 percent annual growth rate even during a period of drastic change. Although reservations and ticketing are done in advance of a flight, seating occurs on a first-come, first-serve basis and is only one illustration of the company's nonconformist practices. Turnaround times are kept to an industry low of 15 minutes with the help of pilots and crew who clean and restock the planes. Refreshments are limited to soft drinks and peanuts, except on its longer flights when cookies and crackers are added to the menu. Southwest does not exchange tickets or baggage with other carriers. Kelleher has noted that if Southwest adopted an assigned seating and computerized, interlining reservation system, ground time would increase enough to necessitate the purchase of at least seven additional airplanes. At a cost of $25 million apiece, the impact on the fares customers pay would be high. Currently, Southwest charges significantly less than its competitors.

CORPORATE PHILOSOPTY, CULTURE, AND HRM PRACTICES

How does Southwest maintain its unique, cost-effective position? In an industry in which antagonistic labor-management relations are common, how does Southwest build cooperation with a work force that is 83 percent unionized? Led by Kelleher, the corporation has developed a culture that treats employees the same way it treats passengers - by paying attention, being responsive, and involving them in decisions.

According to Elizabeth Pedrick Sartain, vice president of People (the company's top HRM person), Southwest's corporate culture makes the airline unique. "We feel this fun atmosphere builds a strong sense of community. It also counterbalances the stress of har worked and competition." As Kelleher has state, "If you don't treat your own people well, they won't treat other people well." So, Southwest's focus is not only on the customer but on the employees, too.

At Southwest, the organizational culture includes a high value on flexibility of the work force. Employees take pride in their ability to get a plane ready to go in only 20 minutes, less than half the industry average. A cultural refrain is "Can't make money with the airplane sitting on the ground." Ramp agents unload baggage, clean the lavatories, carry out trash, and stock the plane with ice, drinks, and peanuts. Flight attendants prepare the cabin for the next flight, and pilots have been known to pitch in when they have time. Working hard is not just an obligation at Southwest; it is a source of pride. Ramp agent Mike Williams brags that in a conversation with an employee for another airline, the other man explained Southwest's fast turnaround by saying, in Williams' words, "The difference is that when one of (the other company's) planes lands, the work it, and when one of our planes lands, we *attack it*."

In addition to the high motivation and expectations for performance, evidence of the company culture can be seen in the recruitment and selection process. Southwest accepts applications for ground operations positions or as flight attendants all year round. Many of the applicants are Southwest customers who've seen recruitment ads like the one featuring Kelleher dressed as Elvis. In 1994, Southwest received more than 126,000 applications for a variety of positions; the People Department interviewed more than 35,000 individuals for 4,500 positions. The expanding company was off to an even faster start the next year; in the first two months of 1995, it hired 1,200 new employees. This large labor pool allows the company to heir employees who most closely fit a culture in which they are asked to use their own judgement and to go beyond "the job description."

CRITICAL THINKING QUESTIONS

1. Describe the Corporate Culture at Southwest Airlines. Be sure to comment on the attitudes of the Southwest employees and the underlying factors that contribute to their feelings.

2. What type of individual does Southwest Airlines seek to recruit and hire?

3. List some techniques used by Southwest that contribute to a positive work environment.

4. Explain the belief that Southwest's competitive strategy of controlling costs through high productivity has contributed to its enormous success.

Journal Entries
Chapter 10 - Human Resource Management

Entry 15:
1. What aspects of HRM have you dealt with in your work experiences?
2. Describe how your performance was appraised on a job or in a class? How was the feedback handled?
3. How does the HRM view of recruitment differ from your view as a job seeker?
4. How were you trained for a job? by your parents? by teachers for the classroom?
5. Are the current methods of performance appraisal used in your classes (or at work) accurate and fair? Explain—including suggestions for improvement if you don't think they're fair.
6. How do you feel about the usefulness of unions? Explain.

Chapter 10

Human Resources Management

Chapter Outline

I.   Training and Development at PepsiCo and Jet

II.   Strategic Human Resource Management
        A.   Components of Human Resource Management
                1.   Recruitment and selection
                2.   Training and development
                3.   Performance appraisal and feedback
                4.   Labor relations
        B.   The Legal Environment of Human Resource Management

III.   Recruitment and Selection
        A.   Human Resource Planning
        B.   Management Insight - Human Resource Planning at Two Small Companies
        C.   Job Analysis
        D.   External and Internal Recruitment
                1.   External recruiting
                2.   Internal recruiting
                3.   Honesty in recruiting
        E.   The Selection Process
                1.   Background information
                2.   Interviews
                3.   Paper and pencil tests
                4.   Physical ability tests
                5.   Performance tests
                6.   References
        F.   Ethics In Action - The Costs of Withholding Negative Information in References
                1.   Reliability
                2.   Validity

IV.   Training and Development
        A.   Types of Training
                1.   Classroom instruction
                2.   Simulations
                3.   On-the-job training
        B.   Types of Development
                1.   Varies work experience
                2.   Formal education

C. Transfer of training and development

V. Performance Appraisal and Feedback
    A. Types of Performance Appraisal
        1. Trait appraisals
        2. Behavior appraisals
        3. Results appraisals
        4. Objective and subjective appraisals
    B. Who Appraises Performance
        1. Self, peers, subordinates, and clients
        2. 360-degree performance appraisals
    C. Effective Performance Feedback

VI. Pay and Benefits
    A. Pay Level
    B. Pay Structure
    C. Benefits
    D. Management Insight - Managing Time with Benefits

VII. Labor Relations
    A. Unions
    B. Focus on Diversity - Linda Chavez-Thompson and the AFL-CIO
    C. Collective Bargaining

Study Questions

<u>True - False Questions</u>

____ 1. Human resource management engages in attracting and retaining employees to ensure performance levels.

____ 2. Selection is the process managers engage in to develop a pool of qualified candidates for open positions.

____ 3. A realistic job preview identifies the tasks, duties, and responsibilities that make up a job.

____ 4. Validity is the degree to which a tool or test measures the same thing each time it is used.

____ 5. Reliability is the degree to which a tool or test measures what it purports to measure.

____ 6. Performance assessment evaluates which employees need training and development and what type of skills or knowledge they need to acquire.

_____ 7.   Performance appraisal is the process managers use to share appraisal information with their subordinates.

_____ 8.   Subjective appraisal is based on traits and behaviors.

_____ 9.   An informal appraisal is unscheduled to check on progress and areas for improvement.

_____ 10. A cafeteria-style plan allows employees to select benefits that are the most advantageous to them.

Multiple Choice Questions

_____ 1.   Equal employment opportunity laws protect against all of the following classes except:
           A.   Age
           B.   Race
           C.   Sexual orientation
           D.   Religion

_____ 2.   _____ is the process managers engage in to develop a pool of qualified candidates for open positions.
           A.   Hiring
           B.   Recruitment
           C.   Retention
           D.   Selection

_____ 3.   The degree to which a tool or test measures what it is supposed to measure is known as:
           A.   validity.
           B.   reliability.
           C.   dependability.
           D.   goodness of fit.

_____ 4.   Preparing organizational members for new responsibilities is referred to as:
           A.   Training
           B.   On-the-job training
           C.   Vertical training
           D.   Development

_____ 5.   _____ appraisal is the evaluation of employees' job performance and contributions to the organization.

A.   Needs
B.   Performance
C.   Assessment
D.   Development

___ 6.   An appraisal based on facts and not traits is an _____ appraisal.
A.   objective
B.   subjective
C.   performance
D.   assessment

___ 7.   A 360-degree appraisal is typically conducted by:
                              I.   Peers
                              II.   Clients
                              III.   Superiors
                              IV.   Subordinates
A.   I, III, IV
B.   I, II, III
C.   II, III, IV
D.   I, II, III, IV

___ 8.   A(n) _____ appraisal is conducted at a set time based on performance measures that were specified in advance.
A.   formal
B.   informal
C.   subjective
D.   objective

___ 9.   The relative position of an organization's pay incentives compared to other companies in the same industry is known as:
A.   pay structure.
B.   pay appraisal.
C.   pay level.
D.   pay feedback.

___ 10.   A plan from which employees can choose the benefits that are the most beneficial to them is called a(n) _____ plan.
A.   informal
B.   cafeteria-style
C.   formal
D.   buffet-style

___ 11.   Collective bargaining may deal with issues such as:
                              I.   Working hours
                              II.   Wages

III. Working conditions
IV. Job security
    A. I, II, III, IV
    B. I, II, III
    C. I, III, IV
    D. II, III, IV

____ 12. Strategic human resource management includes which of these activities in which managers engage:
    I. Utilizing human resources
    II. Attracting human resources
    III. Retaining human resources
    IV. Training human resources
    A. I, II, III, IV
    B. II, III, IV
    C. I, III, IV
    D. I, II, IV

____ 13. Training focuses on:
    A. teaching organizational members how to perform effectively in their current jobs.
    B. broadening organizational members's knowledge and skills.
    C. preparing organizational members to take on new responsibilities.
    D. none of these.

____ 14. In the process of performance feedback:
    A. Managers share performance information with their subordinates.
    B. Managers give subordinates an opportunity to reflect on their own performance.
    C. Managers develop, with the subordinates, plans for the future.
    D. All of these occur.

____ 15. The _____ oversees union activity.
    A. Justice Department
    B. National Labor Relations Board
    C. National Labor Administration Board
    D. Interstate Commerce Commission.

Essay Questions

1. Name the components of a human resource management system.

2. What are the selection tools?

3. In the recruitment and selection system, what function does the job analysis perform?

4. Who appraises performance?

Chapter 10
Human Resource Management

In the corporate offices in Lisle, Illinois, Jack McEnery, the corporate vice-president of training and compensation, and Sylvia McGeachie, vice-president of human resources for Europe, the Middle East, and Africa, were discussing the implementation of the new incentive plan. The plans appeared to be developing smoothly, and both were pleased by the progress they had made in resolving various administrative issues. It was, however, clear from the discussion that neither previous practice nor theory was available to guide their actions. Most organizations have only recently begun to cope with the ambiguous issues that are being discussed by McEnery and McGeachie.

Suddenly, McGeachie became quiet and thoughtful and then said, "You know, Jack, France mandated compulsory profit sharing in 1967 for companies operating within France. This is going to impact our incentive plan. Are we going to factor in this required compensation before the incentives are determined? We certainly don't want to pay for both. That would mean, in effect, a double bonus for managers."

In France, the Law of 1967 enacted mandatory, private profit sharing. Any employer with more than 100 employees must establish a profit-sharing plan within a prescribed framework. The total employees' share in profits is determined at the end of each year. The minimum requirement is that the profit-sharing formula applies to the excess, if any, of the after-tax profit minus 5 percent of invested capital. Allocation is made on the basis of salary. Typically, the profit sharing is distributed in the form of company shares, with a restriction that employees cannot cash these shares for five years.

Budget's incentive plan was designed to support a global strategy that would reward salaried employees for achieving corporate goals. If 70 percent of the corporate goals regarding profitability are reached, there is a payout to all exempt employees. The amount is based both on profit and on the salary grade of the exempt employee. No base pay is at risk; however, considerable additional compensation may be possible when profit goals are achieved. For example, a manager may receive 25 percent of his/her salary immediately and 25 percent after three years. A vice president may receive 40 percent of his/her salary via an immediate payout and an equivalent amount in three years. Twenty percent of the payout relates to the level of total corporate profitability, another 20 percent relates to regional profitability, and 60 percent depends on the achievement of local goals (in this case, France).

Budget's intention was to align pay practices with business strategy and also compensate employees internationally in a fair, comparable manner. The philosophy was that of "think globally, but act locally." Since France had mandated profit sharing, however, several issues occurred to McEnery and McGeachie as they discussed the incentive plan.

BUDGET'S HISTORY

Budget was founded in 1958 by Morris Mirkin and Jules Lederer in a Los Angeles storefront. They began renting Chevys at $4 a day and $.04 a mile. In the mid 1960s, Budget began international operations when it opened operations in Canada and Puerto Rico. Expansion into Great Britain occurred a few years later.

As of 1993, Budget Rent-a-Car is the third largest company in the car rental industry. There are approximately 3,200 locations worldwide (about half are owned by licensees). Sales in 1992 were $2.4 billion, with half of the sales accounted for by licensees. There are 160,000 vehicles available for rent worldwide.

ISSUES IN COMPENSATION

During a continuation of their discussion, McEnery asked McGeachie, "Do you think that with the mandated profit-sharing process in France we can create a sufficiently motivating environment with Budget's incentive plan? I think it is important that we avoid underpayment since that will be frustrating and may be perceived as unfair by employees. On the other hand, overpayment is both inappropriate for Budget and possibly de-motivating. Why, after all, if you already get a high reward for moderate effort make an extraordinary effort?"

"I agree," McGeachie responded, "but I think that if we ensure that the rewards are high enough beyond the legal requirements, motivation will be strong. We must try to ensure in France that approximately the same level of pay related to profit is at risk as in other countries. It is my perception after working a great deal with the French that although historically the government has had a socialistic orientation, there would be few differences among the French managers in how they would react to incentives as compared with other Europeans. French managers have become cosmopolitan in understanding the trends of business across Europe, and incentive compensation is a very important issue right now. We must discuss the issue with our people in France, but I think in this area, at least, we will see similar reactions and motivation."

After some consideration, McEnery suggested, "So we have to consider the factors that might interfere with the level of the reward." "That's right," said McGeachie, "and one critical issue to consider is the income tax rate of the French. Although the income tax also funds health care coverage and pensions, it is very high. There is a rapidly sliding scale based on income, with no deductions allowed except for dependents. For instance, the income tax rate is 50 percent at the American equivalent of approximately $52,000. The same incentive amount will equate to less reward in France as compared with the United States, because of taxes."

"Let me play devil's advocate," said McEnery, "and suggest that while pay is a concern of the company and employee, the income tax rate is the concern of the citizen and the government of a country." (Some compensation specialists believe that the analysis should be pretax; otherwise, every time a government changes the tax structure, the compensation structure of organizations would need revision.)

The discussion was continued later with the marketing manager in France, Bertrand Guidard. Guidard stated, "Employee reactions to incentives will depend, in France, on the level of the employee. Higher-level employees are very concerned about profitability in France since they recognize this relates to the future of Budget in France as well as to their bonus. The incentive plan is very motivating for managers, although I don't believe that lower level employees are motivated by the idea of possible incentives. We need an incentive plan, although it has to be possible to reach."

CONCLUSIONS

In international compensation, there are two forces that must be considered simultaneously. First, there must be a global vision that allows 'in organization to formulate a business strategy that crosses national borders. Many argue that a single marketplace has been created by competitiveness of global operations. Particularly in a service organization, the ability to attract and retain customers is critical. The emphasis on quality in service has become a monumental concern. Poor service may send more customers to your global competition than price or quality.

The second consideration is the impact of local conditions. Culture, and even operations of an international organization, will vary across borders. Therefore, an international compensation decision involves the reinforcement of global strategy but also must recognize and reward differences in cultural approaches. Communication is critical about both basic compensation philosophy and the way goals are set, measured, and rewarded.

The management of human resources may be the key to global success. Compensation strategies therefore need to reinforce the concept of service delivery. The incentive plan described for Budget was designed to maintain the motivation and satisfaction of management employees, as well as to ensure the company's competitive ability to attract and retain the best employees.

DISCUSSION QUESTIONS

1. What do you think Budget should do about the incentive plan in France?

2. Do you think that compensation decisions should be made pre- or post-tax? Defend your position.

3. What should "think globally, act locally" mean when implementing an incentive plan such as Budget's?

4. Put yourself in the position of a manager for Budget. How do you reconcile the issue of government-mandated profit sharing versus additional incentives designed by Budget? Would compensation be likely to affect your behavior or other managers' behavior in different ways?

Journal Entries
Chapter 11 - The Manager as a Person

Entry 16:
1. What are the pro's and con's of being a high self-monitor (which you've experienced)?
2. Which personality traits best fit you and why?
3. Describe your personality in terms of the Big 5 Traits or the listing of traits that affect organizational behavior. Use examples to demonstrate your assessment.
4. Describe your terminal and instrumental values.
5. How satisfied are you with your current job (being a student could be considered a job)? How does that impact your actions? Or do your actions impact your satisfaction?
6. Describe a situation where your perceptions differed from somebody else. How did it impact your interaction with the other person?
7. Describe your expected career path. Will it be linear, steady, or spiral?
8. Describe the career path of your boss or parent.
9. What are your major sources and consequences of stress as a student? How do you cope?

Chapter 11

The Manager as a Person

Chapter Outline

I.   Low-Key determination versus Flamboyant Outspokenness

II.   Enduring Characteristics: Personality Traits
      A.   The Big Five Personality Traits
            1.   Extroversion
            2.   Negative affectivity
            3.   Agreeableness
            4.   Conscientiousness
            5.   Openness to experience
      B.   Focus on Diversity - Openness to Experience Reigns at Any Age
      C.   Other Personality Traits that Affect Managerial Behavior
            1.   Locus of control
            2.   Self-esteem
            3.   Needs for achievement, affiliation, and power

III. Values, Attitudes, and Moods
      A.   Values: Terminal and Instrumental
      B.   Managing Globally - Values of the Overseas Chinese
      C.   Attitudes
            1.   Job satisfaction
            2.   Organizational commitment
      D.   Management Insight - Managerial Commitment at IBM
      E.   Moods

IV.   Perceptions
      A.   Factors that Influence Managerial Perceptions
      B.   Ways to Ensure Accurate Perceptions

V.   Career Development
      A.   Stages in a Linear Career
            1.   Preparation for work
            2.   Organizational entry
            3.   Early career
            4.   Mid-career
            5.   Late career
      B.   Effective Career Management
            1.   Commitment to ethical career practices

2.   Accommodations for workers' multi-dimensional lives

VI.   Stress
    A.   Consequences of Stress
        1.   Physiological consequences
        2.   Psychological consequences
        3.   Behavioral consequences
    B.   Sources of Managerial Stress
    C.   Management Insight - Role Overload Downs Harvard President
    D.   Coping with Stress
        1.   Problem-focused coping
        2.   Emotion-focused coping
        3.   Emotional intelligence

Study Questions

<u>True - False Questions</u>

____ 1.   Extroversion is the tendency to experience positive emotions and moods that makes one feel good about oneself and everyone else.

____ 2.   With an internal locus of control one believes that one's own behavior has little impact on any outcome.

____ 3.   Need for achievement is concerned with needing to be liked and to get along with other people.

____ 4.   Terminal value is a personal conviction about lifelong goals that an individual seeks to achieve.

____ 5.   A feeling or state of mind is called an attitude.

____ 6.   A career consisting of the same kind of job during a large part of one's work life is known as a steady-state career.

____ 7.   A glass ceiling is a position from which the chances of being promoted are slight.

____ 8.   The condition of having too many responsibilities to perform is referred to as role conflict.

____ 9.   Emotion-focused coping are the actions people take to deal with their stressful feelings and emotions.

____ 10.   Emotional support is support provided by other people, such as friends.

Multiple Choice Questions

_____ 1. Negative _____ is the tendency to experience negative emotions and moods and to be critical of oneself and other people.
   A. satisfaction
   B. attitude
   C. affectivity
   D. commitment

_____ 2. _____ is the tendency to be careful, scrupulous, and persevering.
   A. Agreeableness
   B. Conscientiousness
   C. Openness to experience
   D. Self-esteem

_____ 3. One who believes that one's own behavior has little or no impact on outcomes is known as a _____ locus of control.
   A. internal
   B. external
   C. linear
   D. positive

_____ 4. The need for _____ provides an individual with a strong desire to perform challenging tasks well and met personal standards of excellence.
   A. achievement
   B. affiliation
   C. power
   D. Satisfaction

_____ 5. The collection of feelings and beliefs that managers have about their organization as a whole is referred to as:
   A. effectiveness management.
   B. self-esteem.
   C. organizational commitment.
   D. attitude management.

_____ 6. The process through which people select, organize and interpret what they sense to give meaning tot he world around them is called:
   A. mood.
   B. stress.
   C. attitude.
   D. perception.

_____ 7. This is a career consisting of a series of jobs that build on each other but tend to be fundamentally different:

102

A.   Spiral career
B.   Steady-state career
C.   Vertical career
D.   Linear career

___ 8.   _____ is the friction that occurs when expected behaviors are at odds with each
other.
A.   Role overload
B.   Role conflict
C.   Role focus
D.   Role reversal

___ 9.   The actions people take to deal directly with the source of their stress is called
_____ coping.
A.   emotion-focused
B.   role-focused
C.   problem-focused
D.   self-focused

___ 10.   Emotional intelligence helps managers deal with:
A.   Problem-focused coping.
B.   Stress.
C.   Emotion-focused coping.
D.   All of these.

___ 11.   Managers with a ____ level of emotional intelligence are more likely to understand
how they are feeling and to effectively manage with those feelings.
A.   high
B.   low
C.   moderate
D.   negative

___ 12.   Which is **not** one of the big five personality traits?
A.   Agreeableness
B.   Negative affectivity
C.   Introversion
D.   Openness to experience

___ 13.   A ____ value is a personal conviction about lifelong goals and objectives.
A.   attitudinal
B.   terminal
C.   instrumental
D.   personality

_____ 14.   What can affect a manager's perceptions?

                            I.   Values
                            II.   Moods
                            III.   Attitudes

A.   I and II
B.   II and III
C.   I and III
D.   I, II, and III

_____ 15.   Stress has which kind(s) of consequences?
A.   Behavioral
B.   Psychological
C.   Physiological
D.   All of these

Essay Questions

1.   What are the big five personality traits?

2.   Name some positive mood measures at work.

3.   State the stages in a linear career.

4.   How does positive stress and negative stress affect a manager's work performance?

Journal Entries
Chapter 12 - Motivation

Entry 17:
1. Describe the theory that best describes what motivates you.
2. How is motivation used at your university?
3. Which classes are you more motivated for? Why?
4. What could be done to make this (or another class) more motivating?
5. How do you use the theories to motivate others?
6. Describe your goals and how they motivate you.
7. Describe how you used (or can use) operant conditioning to correct or eliminate an undesired behavior of a friend or co-worker.
8. How has social learning impacted your behaviors?

Chapter 12

Motivation

Chapter Outline

I.   Motivating Employees at Eastman Kodak and Mars

II.   The Nature of Motivation
        A.   Intrinsically Motivated Behavior
        B.   Extrinsically Motivated Behavior

III.   Expectancy Theory
        A.   Expectancy
        B.   Instrumentality
        C.   Valence
        D.   Bringing It All Together
        E.   Managing Globally - Motorola Promotes High Motivation in Malaysia

IV.   Need Theories
        A.   Maslow's Hierarchy of Needs
        B.   Alderfer's ERG Theory
        C.   Herzberg's Motivator Hygiene Theory

V.   Equity Theory
        A.   Equity
        B.   Inequity
        C.   Ways to Restore Equity

VI.   Goal Setting Theory

VII.   Learning Theories
        A.   Operant Conditioning Theory
                1.   Positive reinforcement
                2.   Negative reinforcement
                3.   Identifying the right behaviors for reinforcement
                        a.   Management Insight - Positive Reinforcement in Luling, Louisiana
                4.   Extinction
                5.   Punishment
                6.   Organizational behavior modification
        B.   Social Learning Theory
                1.   Vicarious learning
                2.   Self-reinforcement

3. Self-efficacy

VIII. Pay and Motivation
  A. Basing Merit Pay on Individual, Group, or Organizational Performance
  B. Salary Increase or Bonus
  C. Examples of Merit Pay Plans
  D. Management Insight - Semiconductors Simplify the Administration of Piece-Rate Pay

Study Questions

<u>True - False Questions</u>

___ 1. Extrinsically motivated behavior is performed to acquire material or social rewards or to avoid punishment.

___ 2. Valence in expectancy theory is how desirable each of the outcomes available from a job or organization is to a person.

___ 3. Maslow proposed that the highest level of unmet needs is the prime motivator and that more than one level of needs is constantly motivational.

___ 4. The theory of motivation that focuses on the fairness of work outcomes relative to work inputs in referred to as equity theory.

___ 5. Underpayment inequity exists when a person perceives that his or her own outcome/input is less than or equal to the ratio of a referent.

___ 6. Equity theory focuses on identifying the types of goals that are the most effective in producing high levels of motivation and performance and explaining why goals have these effects.

___ 7. Operant conditioning theory states that people learn to perform behaviors that lead to desired consequences and learn not to perform behaviors that lead to undesired consequences.

___ 8. Negative reinforcement is administering an undesired or negative consequence when dysfunctional behavior occurs.

___ 9. Self-learning theory takes into account how learning and motivation are influenced by people's thoughts and beliefs and their observations of other people's behavior.

___ 10. Self-efficacy is a person's belief about his or her ability to perform a behavior successfully.

Multiple Choice Questions

___ 1.   Motivation consists of psychological forces that determine all but which of these:
- A.   The direction of a person's behavior in an organization.
- B.   A person's level of effort.
- C.   A person's level of persistence.
- D.   A person's desire for success.

___ 2.   In expectancy theory, _____ is a perception about the extent of which effort will result in a certain level of performance.
- A.   effort
- B.   expectancy
- C.   valence
- D.   instrumentality

___ 3.   _____ in expectancy theory is a perception about the extent to which performance will result in the attainment of outcomes.
- A.   Expectancy
- B.   Valence
- C.   Instrumentality
- D.   Effort

___ 4.   This theory states that three universal needs for existence, relatedness, and growth constitute a hierarchy of needs and motivates behavior:
- A.   Alderfer's ERG Theory
- B.   Herzberg's Motivator Hygiene Theory
- C.   Scheid's Goal-Setting Theory
- D.   Equity Theory

___ 5.   Which of the following has a different approach from the other two?
- A.   Alderfer's ERG Theory
- B.   Herzberg;'s Motivator Hygiene Theory
- C.   Maslow's Hierarchy of Needs
- D.   None of these

___ 6.   _____ arranges five basic needs to motivate behavior.
- A.   Maslow's Hierarchy of Needs
- B.   Alderfer's ERG Theory
- C.   Herzberg's Motivator Hygiene Theory
- D.   Scheid's Goal-Setting Theory

___ 7.   Inequity that exists when a person perceives that his or her own outcome/input ratio is greater than the ratio of a referent is known as:

A. underpayment inequity
B. overpayment inequity
C. negative perception inequity
D. equivalency inequity

___ 8.   Theories that focus on increasing employee motivation and performance by linking outcomes that employees receive to the performance of desired behaviors and the attainment of goals are called _____ theories.
A. operant
B. goal-setting
C. learning
D. equity

___ 9.   Curtailing the performance of dysfunctional behaviors by eliminating whatever reinforces them is known as:
A. negative reinforcement.
B. positive reinforcement.
C. punishment.
D. extinction.

___ 10.   _____ learning occurs when the learner becomes motivated to perform a behavior by watching another person perform it.
A. Social
B. Positive
C. Vicarious
D. Negative

___ 11.   _____ is any desired or attractive outcome or reward that a person gives to himself or herself for good performance.
A. Self-reinforcer
B. Self-motivator
C. Self-learner
D. Self-efficacy

___ 12.   According to expectancy theory, managers can promote high levels of motivation in their organization by taking steps to insure that:
I.   Expectancy is high
II.   Instrumentality is high
III.   Effort is high
IV.   Valence is high
A. I, II, III, IV
B. I, II, III
C. II, III, IV
D. I, II, IV

___ 13.   In goal-setting theory it is important for organizational people to do all of these except:
A.   Set the goals
B.   Accept the goals
C.   Be committed to the goals
D.   Receive feedback about their performance.

___ 14.   Managers can motivate people to avoid performing dysfunctional behaviors by using:
I.   Extinction
II.   Punishment
III.   Negative reinforcement
A.   I, II, III
B.   I and III
C.   II and III
D.   I and II

___ 15.   Merit pay plans can be based on:
A.   Individual performance
B.   Group performance
C.   Organizational performance
D.   All of these.

Essay Questions

1.   What are expectancy, instrumentality and valence?

2.   How is high motivation achieved in expectancy theory?

3.   From lowest to highest, what are Maslow's Hierarchy of Needs?

4.   Utilizing Alderfer's ERG Theory, what are the lowest-level needs to the highest needs?

Chapter 12
Motivation

It's important to understand the reasons why effective managers must be concerned with employee motivation. After identifying some of the factors contributing to motivation, this video looks at how Tellabs, Inc., has successfully applied motivation theory.

Tellabs is based in the Chicago area, but is internationally known for its telecommunications products and services. However, recently the company gained fame when its stock increased 1,683 percent over a five-year period, making Tellabs the best performing stock at that time on the New York Stock Exchange, the American Stock Exchange, and NASDAQ. Tellabs was founded in 1975 by a group of engineers brainstorming at a kitchen table, and grew from 20 employees with annual sales of $312,000 to 2,600 employees with annual sales of $494 million in 1994. Tellabs currently designs, manufactures, markets, and services voice and data transport and network access systems.

One of the principal reasons for Tellabs' remarkable success has been its ability to motivate its workforce. In simple terms, employee motivation refers to an employee's willingness to perform in his or her job. Effective managers must be concerned with motivating employees toward common goals that will improve the success of the company. At Tellabs, a motivated workforce has enhanced the quality of its products and services.

Tellabs' manager of quality, Joe Taylor, explains what's behind the company's motivated workers: "In the past 10 years we've found that to improve our quality we had to invest in our employees through training programs. Specifically, they have the tools and the resources now to make a difference within our processes in the factory and provide us with process improvements."

A motivated workforce contributes to increased quality in goods and services, greater efficiency in work processes, and improved customer service. Grace Pastiak said, "When I look at the improvements that Tellabs has made since implementing just-in-time and Total Quality Commitment, by far the biggest gain has been exciting employees to do their best and giving them the opportunity to implement their own ideas."

At its core, motivation results from an individual's desire to satisfy personal needs or goals. Every person has set of needs or goals that influences their behavior. Abraham Maslow postulated that needs can be placed in a hierarchy and that as each need level in the hierarchy is satisfied, the person will concentrate on meeting needs at the next level.

Frederick Herzberg conducted a study in the 1960s that concluded that factors pertaining to the work itself, such as achievement, recognition, and responsibility, tended to actually motivate employees. Other factors, such as supervision, pay, and company policies, might increase job satisfaction, but not necessarily employee motivation.

A third approach to motivation, developed by McGregor, involves two opposing theories about the nature of human behavior. Theory X holds that some employees are lazy, or unwilling to work unless motivated by negative factors such as threats and constant supervision. Theory Y holds that employees want to work and do a good job and are motivated best by incentives, responsibility, and ownership of their work.

Maslow's hierarchy, Herzberg's factors, and McGregor's theories suggest that it's in a company's best interest to offer employees adequate rewards and to appeal to their pride of ownership. At Tellabs, many employees say that the entrepreneurial atmosphere - nurtured by managers makes them feel good about themselves. So Tellabs clearly takes a Theory Y approach.

Effective managers help create a work environment that encourages, supports, and sustains improvement in work performance. At Tellabs, mangers have implemented job rotation systems and a cadre of high performance teams to help enrich jobs and create an innovative working environment. Another innovation at Tellabs to ensure a high level of employee motivation is high performance teams.

Some companies may use a combination of motivation theories. In 1992, Tellabs presented its corporate goals, known as Strategic Initiatives, to its employees. The corporate mission statement emphasized the company's goals, quality, customer satisfaction, profits, growth, its people, and its corporate integrity.

Tellabs' total compensation plan includes air Employee Stock Option Plan and retirement investments, such as 401(k). Also employees receive an annual bonus based on the company's productivity.

At Tellabs, employee motivation and performance are enhanced by an atmosphere in which employees are openly told they are valued and trusted. Managers encourage calculated risk taking and innovation. They empower workers through cross-functional teams so that they are able to identify problems and develop effective solutions.

Tellabs' Career Development System trains internal candidates for key management positions, while its competitive compensation plan shares the wealth, contributes to employee satisfaction, and encourages peak performance.

CRITICAL THINKING QUESTIONS

1. McGregor's Theory X and Theory Y have totally different views of the typical worker. Which of the two theories do you think managers should adopt? Explain. Describe how adopting Theory X would affect a manager's behavior toward employees. Do the same for Theory Y.

2. What are some of the potential pitfalls of' using employee empowerment as a motivational device in the workplace?

3.   Herzberg's theory says workplace factors lead to employee motivation. What are some workplace factors not mentioned in the video that could affect employee motivation?

Journal Entries
Chapter 13 - Leadership

Entry 18:
1. Describe your personal leadership style, or the style of your boss. How do others respond to the style? Are you a leader or follower? Formally or informally?
2. What leadership style do you use? Why?
3. What leadership style best describes your boss? Is it the most effective?
4. Which style best describes the student-teacher relationship?
5. Select a historically "great leader" and describe what about his/her leadership style made him/her worth remembering.

Entry 19:
1. Describe your (or your boss's) sources of power. Is it personal or position based power? Is it the same in all situations?
2. Describe a charismatic leader you know personally. How much influence does this individual have on you? on others?
3. How have the male and female bosses (or teachers) differed in their leadership approaches? Which was the most effective?
4. Do you delegate or assign tasks? Which does your boss do?

Chapter 13

Leadership

Chapter Outline

I.   Welch Fosters Prosperity While Agee Fosters Decline

II.   The Nature of Leadership
    A.   Personal Leadership Style and Managerial Tasks
    B.   Leadership Styles Across Cultures
    C.   Power: The Key to Leadership
        1.   Legitimate power
        2.   Reward power
        3.   Coercive power
            a.   Ethics In Action - Curtailing Coercive Power Makes Good Business Sense
        4.   Expert power
        5.   Referent power
    D.   Empowerment - An Ingredient in Modern Management

III.   Trait and Behavior Models of Leadership
    A.   The Trait Model
    B.   The Behavior Model
        1.   Consideration
            a.   Management Insight - Consideration and Customer Service
            b.   Initiating structure

IV.   Contingency models of Leadership
    A.   Fiedler's Contingency Model
        1.   Leader style
        2.   Situational characteristics
        3.   Leader-member relations
        4.   Task structure
        5.   Position power
        6.   Combining leader style and the situation
        7.   Putting the contingency model into practice
    B.   House's Path - Goal Theory
        1.   Ascertain the outcomes subordinates desire from their jobs and the organization
        2.   Reward subordinates for high performance and achieving goals
        3.   Clarify the paths to goal attainment, remove obstacles to high performance, and express confidence in subordinates capabilities

C. Management Insight - Turnarounds in the Steel Industry
D. The Leader Substitutes Model
E. Bringing It All Together

V. Transformational Leadership
   A. Being a Charismatic Leader
   B. Stimulating Subordinates Intellectually
   C. Engaging in Developmental Consideration
   D. Managing Globally - Transformational Leadership in South Korea
   E. The Difference Between Transformational and Transactional Leadership
      1. Gender and leadership
      2. Female managers

Study Questions

True - False Questions

____ 1. Reward power is the ability of a manager to give or withhold tangible and intangible rewards.

____ 2. Exclusive power is based in the special knowledge, skills, and expertise that a leader possesses.

____ 3. Initiating structure managerial behavior to insure that work gets done, subordinates perform their jobs acceptably, and the organization is efficient and effective.

____ 4. Relationship-oriented leaders have a primary concern to develop good relationships with their subordinates and to be liked by them.

____ 5. Task-oriented leaders have a primary concern to insure the organization performs at a high level.

____ 6. Functional power is a determinant of how favorable a situation is for leading.

____ 7. An enthusiastic leader able to clearly communicate a vision of how good things could be is known as a charismatic leader.

____ 8. Managers are using empowerment as a tool to increase their effectiveness as leaders.

____ 9. Some managers who possess the traits of trait model leadership are not effective leaders, while some who do not posses all the traits are effective leaders.

_____ 10. Female and male managers differ in leadership behaviors that they perform.

Multiple Choice Questions

_____ 1. The authority a manager has by virtue of his or her position in an organization is referred to as ____ power.
  A. legitimate
  B. reward
  C. coercive
  D. expert

_____ 2. This is the ability of a manager to punish others:
  A. Coercive power
  B. Exclusive power
  C. Command power
  D. Referent power

_____ 3. _____-oriented leaders are leaders whose primary concern is to develop good relationships with their subordinates and to be liked by them.
  A. Leader-member
  B. Task
  C. Initiating
  D. Relationship

_____ 4. The extent to which followers like, trust, and are loyal to their leader is called:
  A. Leadership relations
  B. Leader-member relations
  C. Empowerment relations
  D. Relationship relations

_____ 5. The ____ structure is a determinant of favorable a situation is for leading.
  A. leadership
  B. path
  C. task
  D. function

_____ 6. The path - goal theory of leadership proposes that leaders can motivate subordinates by which of these:
        I.   Identifying their desired outcomes
        II.   Rewarding high performance and goal attainment
        III. Creating the paths leading to goal attainment
  A. I and II
  B. I and III
  C. II and III

D.   I, II, and III

___ 7.   Leadership that makes subordinates aware of the importance of their jobs to the organization and their own need for personal growth is referred to as:
A.   Task-oriented leadership
B.   Transformational leadership
C.   Charismatic leadership
D.   Relationship leadership

___ 8.   _____ leadership motivates subordinates by rewarding high performance and reprimanding low performance.
A.   Task-oriented
B.   Transformational
C.   Transactional
D.   Transnational

___ 9.   Which of these is **not** a type of power available to a manager?
A.   Reward
B.   Expert
C.   referent
D.   Command

___ 10.   Which is **not** a kind of behavior managers can engage in to motivate subordinates:
A.   Directive behaviors
B.   Participative behaviors
C.   Assessment-oriented behaviors
D.   Supportive behaviors

___ 11.   Transformational leadership occurs in all of these except when:
A.   Managers have dramatic effects on their subordinates
B.   Managers have an effect on the industry as a whole
C.   Managers inspire subordinates
D.   Managers improve performance

___ 12.   Managers can engage in transformational leadership by being:
        I.   Charismatic leaders
        II.   Engaging in development consideration
        III.   Intellectually stimulating subordinates
A.   I and II
B.   II and III
C.   I and III
D.   I, II, and III

___ 13.   Which contingency model describes two leader styles and the situations in which

each leader will be the most effective?
A.   Fiedler's
B.   House's
C.   Leader Substitutes
D.   Vest's

____ 14.   This contingency model describes how effective leaders motivate their followers:
A.   Vest's
B.   House's
C.   Fiedler's
D.   Leader Substitutes

____ 15.   The _____ model describes when leadership is unnecessary.
A.   Fiedler's
B.   House's
C.   Leader Substitutes
D.   Vest's

Essay Questions

1.   What is the key contingency of House's Path - Goal Theory?

2.   According to the Leader Substitute Model, whether or not leadership is necessary is contingent upon what factors?

3.   Describe a transformational manager.

4.   Effective leaders exhibit what traits?

Chapter 13
Leadership

An organization must have leadership at even level in order to succeed. Leaders must tailor their leadership skills based on their assessment of their tasks and their followers. At Marshall Industries, one of the top five electronics distributors in North America, leaders include the founder and the president of the company, as well as the warehouse manager and an entry-level warehouse employee. The diversity of these leaders' skills illustrates that different skills are appropriate to each situation within an organization.

Managers need to understand essential definitions and concepts related to leadership in the workplace. Leadership is providing direction, energizing others, and obtaining commitment to a cause. For leadership to take place a group must have a task, job, or assignment to be performed or a quality to be achieved, one or more leaders, and, of course, followers.

The skills and behaviors of effective leaders vary with the nature of the job to be done, the behavior of the followers, and the leader's style and behavior. Leadership situations within organizations are usually a combination of: visionary/pathfinding, problem solving, and implementing.

Marshall Industries is one of the largest electronics distributors in the United States. The company has enjoyed tremendous success over the past ten years. During this time, Marshall has evolved away from a results-oriented, internally competitive mode of employee accountability toward a team-centered focus on quality through continuous process improvement. New demands have been made upon Marshall's existing leadership, and new leaders have emerged at all levels of the company.

Gordon Marshall, the founder and chief executive officer of Marshall Industries, exemplifies the characteristics of the visionary/pathfinder leader. Visionary/pathfinder leaders usually emerge at the top level of an organization. Their leadership role is to create a vision of future possibilities and influence others to share it. Gordon Marshall faced perhaps his biggest leadership challenge at an unusual point in his career. As he stated, "I came back to the company in February of 1982. I was semiretired. The company was losing money, so I decided to come back and see if I could fix it."

Several years after his return, Marshall spotted an article about W. Edwards Deming's quality principles - an article that would eventually have a major impact at Marshall Industries. Marshall said, "The things that really hit me, struck me as being so fundamental: One: Listen to the voice of the customer. Two: Improve the quality of your product or service and then have a process that continues to improve those things on an ongoing basis. Three: Do it right the first time and take the cost out of the process so you can become the lowest cost producer. Produce the highest quality and do the best job of servicing the customer."

Robert Rodin, the president and chief operating officer of Marshall Industries, remembers the beginnings of Gordon Marshall's vision. Rodin said, "About three and a half years ago Gordon read an article on Dr. Deming and his 14 points and he showed it to myself and Dick gently.

While very concise, it was difficult to understand and we began to really wrestle with the concepts. We met with some people and we attended the Deming four-day seminar and began to get a picture of what this possibly could mean for the company."

Gordon Marshall's leadership role as visionary/pathfinder was to point out a possible way to go and to mobilize commitment. The visionary/pathfinder leaves it to others to study, refine, and implement their vision. Rodin has functioned in a dual leadership role at Marshall Industries. He's shared the role of visionary/pathfinder with Gordon Marshall, but he's also been the problem solver and implementer of strategies and practices that will realize the initial vision. As he put it, "In the past, in my role in the company I was really focusing a lot on administrative details, refereeing, cheerleading, and making sure our company was dealing with the fires of the day. Our thinking was basically short term. In the new system, my responsibilities are very different. We're not in a functional organization where the job of everybody who works for me is to make me happy, but rather to build the best process to achieve our mission. So, in this new role, I have to facilitate continuous improvement and eliminate barriers. I have to provide vision into the future in the strategic nature of our business and work with our employees very frequently on a peer level to understand and make sure that they understand their jobs and find ways that I can facilitate continuous improvement and innovation for them."

Leadership occurs not just at the top management level of an organization but wherever there is a group or team task. That means almost any organizational situation. Warehouse Manager Mike Lelo is another leader at Marshall Industries. His leadership role is that of problem solver. Like President Rodin, Lelo tailors his leadership role to the situation and to the behavior of his followers. Lelo said, "Marshall deals with over 200 suppliers and 200,000 parts companies. We have about 30,000 customers. To operate this whole thing, we have to employ about 140 people. I'll never go out and say this is exactly how this is to be done because, guess what, it changes again every day. There are things that are going to be different. I could never get out and be involved in such detail in every department where I'm directing everybody what to do. I have them come back to me and say 'this is what I am doing.' Then we'll analyze something, think about it, and make sure we're doing the right things. But I'll never say 'Go out and do this.'"

"The moment a person is hired at Marshall's they go through an orientation that shows them all about the company in general. When they come into the warehouse, we don't just say 'Go into the first department that you're assigned to and that's where you're going to stay when you work here.' We tour the whole facility, we show them all the operations and how they interconnect - how receiving sends parts to storage, how storage goes to picking and special handling, and so forth. And they start to see the whole wheel that's spinning."

Lelo is not concerned with conceiving or implementing a vision for Marshall Industries' future, but with solving immediate and incipient problems that occur in the company's central warehouse. As Mike Lelo and his followers address and solve these problems his style is supportive and facilitative. He helps them articulate goals and the paths to obtain those goals. His followers are self-assured. Lelo's leadership style seems to work because of his good interpersonal relationships with his team members as well as their acceptance of responsibility and their maturity. His relationship-based style of leadership works well at the warehouse at Marshall Industries with its eager, mature supervisors.

At Marshall Industries, leaders include Gordon Marshall, a visionary/pathfinder, Robert Rodin a visionary/pathfinder and implementer, and Mike Lelo, an implementer and problem solver. Their leadership skills differ, but each is appropriate to their specific leadership challenge. Each has found that the needs of the organization have shaped their leadership style and each can expect that the demands of leadership will demand additional changes in the future.

DISCUSSION QUESTIONS

1. What are the behaviors of the leaders at Marshall Industries? What are the results in terms of employee motivation, satisfaction, and productivity?

2. The video states that leadership is a combination of visionary pathfinder, problem-solver, and implementer. Explain how each of the following managers at Marshall exemplifies these behaviors.
    *   Gordon Marshall (Founder)
    *   Robert Rodin (President and CEO)
    *   Michael Lelo (Warehouse Manager)

3. Humberto Hernandez is an informal leader at Marshall. Why is he recognized as being an informal leader and what does he do in this role?

4. According to Rob Rodin, what are the key elements of his leadership role now at Marshall Industries? What was his role before the company's transformation?

5. Rob Rodin, President and Chief Executive Officer, believes part of his job is to work with employees on a peer level. Comment on what this means. Do you agree this is necessary or is it best left to lower-level managers and supervisors?

Journal Entries
Chapter 14 - Groups and Teams

Entry 20:

1. What groups do you belong to? How do they differ? How are they alike?
2. How have your group projects at your university reflected the team concepts discussed?
3. Have you ever been a member of a highly cohesive group? What made it cohesive? How did it impact the group's activities?
4. Do you think cohesiveness is good or bad? Cite personal examples to support your view.
5. Have you ever experienced peer pressure to act more in accordance to the behavioral norms of a group? What happened?
6. Have you ever engaged in social loafing? What do you do when another member of your group is trying to engage in social loafing?

Chapter 14

Groups and Teams

Chapter Outline

I. Teams Work Wonders at Hallmark Cards

II. Groups, Teams, and Organizational Effectiveness
    A. Groups and Teams as Performance Enhancers
    B. Groups and Teams, and Responsiveness to Customers
    C. Management insight - Teams Foster Responsiveness to Customers at Rubbermaid
    D. Teams and Innovation
    E. Managing Globally - Cross-Cultural Team's Innovation Yields the 1996 Honda Civic
    F. Groups and Teams as Motivators

III. Types of Groups and Teams
    A. The Top Management Team
    B. Research and Development Teams
    C. Command Groups
    D. Task Forces
    E. Self-Managed Work teams
    F. Virtual Teams
    G. Friendship Groups
    H. Interest Groups

IV. Group Dynamics
    A. Group Size, Tasks, and Roles
        1. Size
        2. Tasks
        3. Pooled task interdependence
        4. Sequential task interdependence
        5. Reciprocal task interdependence
        6. Roles
    B. Group Leadership
    C. Group Development Over Time
        1. Forming
        2. Storming
        3. Norming
        4. Performing
        5. Adjourning
    D. Group Norms

1.　　Conformity and deviance
　　　2.　　Encouraging a balance of conformity and deviance
　　E.　　Group Cohesiveness
　　　1.　　Consequences of group cohesiveness
　　　2.　　Level of participation within a group
　　　3.　　Level of conformity to group norms
　　　4.　　Emphasis on group goal accomplishment
　　　5.　　Factors leading to group cohesiveness
　　　　a.　　Size
　　　　b.　　Effectively managed diversity
　　　　　i.　　Focus on Diversity - Promoting Cohesiveness in a Diverse Team at Mercedes Benz
　　　　c.　　Group identity and healthy competition
　　　　d.　　Success

V.　　Managing Groups and Teams for High Performance
　　A.　　Motivating Group Members to Achieve Organizational Goals
　　B.　　Management Insight - Rewarding Team Members
　　C.　　Reducing Social Loafing in Groups
　　　1.　　Make individual contributions identifiable
　　　2.　　Emphasize the valuable contributions of individual members
　　　3.　　Keep group size at an appropriate level
　　D.　　Helping Groups Manage Conflict Effectively

Study Questions

<u>True - False Questions</u>

____ 1.　　Two or more people who interact with each other to accomplish a goal is called a group.

____ 2.　　A formal group is one that individuals establish to achieve organizational goals.

____ 3.　　A top-management team is composed of the CEO and the heads of all departments.

____ 4.　　A friendship group rarely if ever meets.

____ 5.　　An interest group is an informal group composed of employees who share similar interests and like to socialize together.

____ 6.　　Task interdependence that exists when the work performed by each group member is completely dependent on the work performed by other group members is referred to as reciprocal task interdependence.

127

___ 7.   Social loafing is the tendency of individuals to put forth less effort when they work in groups.

___ 8.   Informal groups by definition do not need leadership.

___ 9.   Managers should form groups with no more members than are needed to provide the group with the human resources it needs to achieve its goals and use a division of labor.

___ 10.   To be effective, groups need a balance of conformity and deviance.

Multiple Choice Questions

___ 1.   A group whose members work intensely with each other to achieve a specific common goal is known as a:
            A.   group.
            B.   team.
            C.   formal group.
            D.   force.

___ 2.   A command group is also known as a(n):
                        I.   Unit
                        II.   Division
                        III.   Department
            A.   I and III
            B.   I and II
            C.   II and III
            D.   I, II, and III

___ 3.   A task force is also known as a(n) ___ committee.
            A.   command group
            B.   formal
            C.   formal group
            D.   task

___ 4.   A virtual team may use which of these to meet:
                        I.   Telephone
                        II.   Faxes
                        III.   E-mail
                        IV.   Video conferences
            A.   I, II, and III
            B.   II, III, and IV
            C.   I, II, III, and IV
            D.   None of these

_____ 5.   This is a team whose members rarely if ever meet:
A.   Friendship group
B.   Virtual team
C.   Interest group
D.   Informal group

_____ 6.   _____ is the degree to which the work performed by one member of a group influences the work performed by the other members.
A.   Task interdependence
B.   Pooled task interdependence
C.   Sequential task interdependence
D.   Reciprocal task interdependence

_____ 7.   The task interdependence that exists when group members must perform specific tasks in a predetermined order is known as _____ interdependence.
A.   task
B.   pooled task
C.   sequential task
D.   reciprocal task

_____ 8.   A set of behaviors and tasks that a member of a group is expected to perform because of his or her position in the group is called a group:
A.   norm.
B.   synergy.
C.   cohesiveness.
D.   role.

_____ 9.   Groups and teams can contribute to organizational effectiveness by:
              I.   Enhancing performance
              II.   Motivating others
              III.   Increasing innovation
              IV.   Increasing customer responsiveness
A.   I, II, III, IV
B.   I, II, IV
C.   I, III, IV
D.   III and IV

_____ 10.   Which is a type of group or team?
              I.   Virtual teams
              II.   Command groups
              III.   Cross-organizational teams
              IV.   Self-development teams
A.   I, II, III
B.   I and II
C.   I, III, IV

D. I, II, III, IV

___ 11. Informal groups include:
I.   Self-managed groups
II. Interest groups
III. Friendship groups
A. I, II, III
B. I and II
C. II and III
D. I and III

___ 12. Which is **not** a key element of group dynamics:
A. Group size
B. Group development
C. Group competition
D. Group norms

___ 13. What is the correct order of the five stages of group development?
I.   Adjourning
II. Performing
III. Storming
IV. Forming
V.   Norming
A. IV, III, V, II, I
B. IV, V, III, II, I
C. V, IV, III, II, I
D. IV, III, II, V, I

___ 14. As group cohesiveness increases so to does all but which of these:
A. Level of participation
B. Level of communication
C. Level of conformity to group norms
D. Emphasis on individual goals

___ 15. Which is **not** a type of task interdependence?
A. Pooled
B. Pyramidal
C. Sequential
D. Reciprocal

<u>Essay Questions</u>

1. What are the contributions to organizational effectiveness of groups and teams?

2. What is the order of the stages of group development?

3. Describe the factors leading to group cohesiveness.

4. What are the three ways to reduce social loafing?

Chapter 14
Groups and Teams

Foreign competition is increasing in almost every industry, and so are operating costs. Many industries have found that quality management is the solution to both of these challenges. As a result, a quality movement is sweeping across America. Teamwork is a significant part of this movement. Originally embraced by manufacturing industries, quality management and teamwork are now being used in many service industries as well. Service businesses appreciate the positive effect these practices have on employee morale, productivity, and customer satisfaction.

The University of Michigan Hospitals adopted quality management as a way to attract and keep top people in the health care profession. John Forsyth, Executive Director of the University of Michigan Hospitals, explained, "The three reasons the University of Michigan has become involved in total quality are: number one, to become the provider of choice; number two, to become pre-eminent in education in the medical sciences; and number three, to become the employer of choice. The key here is to have a diverse and motivated work force, and we believe total quality will empower people to that end."

The development of problem solving teams comprised of both managers and employees is one highly effective aspect of a quality program. Team problem solving techniques are proving to be a simple, effective catalyst to organizational creativity, quality improvement, and higher quality of work life. But team building in the United States requires a major culture change. Working in groups is somewhat unnatural to Americans who are instilled with a philosophy of individual achievement beginning in elementary school and continuing throughout their academic and business careers. Larry Warren, an administrator at the University of Michigan Hospitals, expressed his personal reservations about changing to a team oriented culture: "To suggest that we change the way we do business to one of team approach to everything that we do and do in the future, stressed me out a little bit."

For teamwork to be effective, new work relationships must be based on trust. One important way to establish this trust is through extensive training and team skills. Ellen Gaucher, Senior Associate Hospital Director, said, "We were very concerned about pushing people too hard. We thought they might think this was just another thing administration had up their sleeve for making them work harder. So we got involved with developing a training program that we thought would be the hook for us, would get them excited about total quality. And it has worked very well."

When a quality team is initially selected, it should include decision makers from several key groups: employees, peers, senior managers, customers, suppliers, and staff support. The common characteristics of any team member are interest in the team, and the ability to make decisions and commitments on behalf of the team. Joan Robinson, Director of Ambulatory Care Nursing, said, "Our nurses are next to the action. They know what our problems are, and they have been schooled on a scientific process of how to address problems. The total quality approach gives us some of the answers in terms of tools that they can use, and working with other people to solve problems, both clinical and some of the problems in the systems of how we get things done here."

Leadership is crucial for a team approach to be effective. The biggest part of a team leader's job is to keep the team together while its members solve the problem. This means developing critical thinking skills in other team members by asking open ended questions, or by providing business information so decisions can be made. A team leader must know when to intervene and when to stand back. The leader must avoid the temptation to jump in with solutions, allowing the team to solve the problem it has been charged with. Essentially, there are seven ground rules for effective teamwork:

1. *Time control:* Each team should have a clear, achievable deadline for resolving the problem;
2. *Be sensitive:* Each team member should be sensitive to the other members' needs *and expressions;*
3. *Relaxed atmosphere:* An informal, relaxed atmosphere should be fostered;
4. *Be Prepared:* Material needed for team meetings should be prepared in advance;
5. *Qualified and Interested Members:* All team members should be qualified and have an interest in the problem the team has been assigned to solve;
6. *Keep Good Records:* Minutes should be kept of all team meetings; and
7. *Assess Team Performance:* Each team should periodically stop and assess its performance.

When a company develops a quality management program, it's important to implement it slowly and in stages. Widespread team mania at the startup of a quality program can be dangerous. Leadership by example, employee involvement, and team building pilot projects make the transition to team problem solving easier. After training began at the University of Michigan Hospitals, for example, management looked for an area of the hospital to pilot the new team approach. The admitting/discharge unit was selected because of its convoluted system. After examining the problem, the quality team came up with a solution: use a computer link between admitting and housekeeping. Mary Decker Staples, Associate hospital Administrator, said, "It was successful enough that when we initiated measuring how long it was taking us to admit patients we were averaging two hours after the patient was ready to go up to the room to actually get to the room. Last year the average was 24 minutes—a 65 percent reduction in the amount of time it takes to admit a patient."

This early success with the team approach built momentum for the future. Employees gained confidence that the approach was effective. Sally Ellis, Clinical Nurse, remarked, "I think the pilot program that we had with the admissions/discharge team has definitely helped. Some of the things that have come out after it is that we've all had an understanding now of what people do. It takes away some of the myths or perceptions of why something didn't happen. I think that prior to this it was easy to blame someone else why something didn't get done or why a patient didn't get out of here on time."

Once a pilot program has been implemented and employees begin to get excited about the new approach, quality teams can effectively solve all kinds of problems. At the University of Michigan Hospitals, another team tackled problems in accounts receivable. It found that the accounting department was receiving 200 to 300 calls a day-a volume so large that staff members were able to answer less than 50 percent of all calls. The quality team developed more effective means of bookkeeping, which freed up the staff so they were able to handle more calls. Pamela Chapelle, Assistant Manager of Financial Services, said, "For June, the number of calls that we answered was 74 percent. We have never, in the four years that I've been in this department, answered 74 percent of the calls that have come in."

Another quality team helped open up communication between departments for more effective patient care. A pharmacy team was reviewing the administration of drugs by the medical staff when it found that one drug could be administered on an eight hour basis instead of the current six hour basis. The team organized educational sessions with the medical and pharmacy staffs. Michael Ryan, Assistant Director of Pharmacy said "What we find now is that 97 percent of prescribing is being done is on an eight hour basis. This has resulted in savings of labor for staff that have to compound and administer the extra dose as well as the expense of the drug which is a savings of about $30,000 per year."

The key element in effective team problem solving is employee empowerment. Teams cannot be effective if management changes or ignores the team's final recommendations. In a team situation, management must give employees wide latitude in how they go about achieving the company's goals. This requires turning the organizational chart upside down, recognizing that management is there to aid the worker in overcoming problems that arise. True employee empowerment enables an employee to achieve his or her highest potential, which benefits the company and the customer.

The success of quality teams at the University of Michigan Hospitals has been recognized throughout the health care profession. In 1990, Witt and Associates, Inc., and the Health Care Forum awarded the University of Michigan Hospitals with the Commitment to Quality Award. The award was established in 1987 to recognize health care professionals committed to quality health care services. The success of the teamwork approach at the University of Michigan Hospitals has convinced many managers that it is a worthwhile endeavor. Staples said, "I think one of the biggest advantages and positive aspects of total quality is our opportunity to use the knowledge that people who are working at the front line have about what works and what doesn't work. So often we as managers sit back thinking we know what's going on. And when you begin to ask employees what's going on you get a very different picture of the process."

The employees at the University of Michigan Hospitals have embraced the philosophy of quality management, and the use of teams for solving problems, increasing work effort, and developing good employee attitudes. Not only do teams solve problems more effectively, but they also allow the employees to focus on improving the processes that affect them. The result? Smoother working relationships, streamlined procedures, and reduced costs.

CRITICAL THINKING QUESTIONS

1. Producing quality services through the use of teamwork has proven an effective approach for the University of Michigan Hospitals. Why do you think team problem solving has proven to be so effective? How do teams differ from committees or task forces?

2. As discussed briefly in the video, some employees will initially resist organizational transformation to a team approach. Why do you think employees would resist this change? What are some techniques a manager might use to help overcome this resistance?

3. Teams are very effective in solving problems related to the process flow of an organization. Try to think of some organizational problems or issues that are not likely to be resolved using a team approach. Explain why you think so.

Journal Entries
Chapter 15 - Communication

Entry 21:

1. Describe a problem that developed due to your poor communication. How did you fix it?

2. When there is a discrepancy between someone's verbal and non-verbal communications, which do you "believe"? Why?

3. How have your perceptions impacted your ability to communicate effectively? Where does it impact you most--as the receiver or sender of the message?

4. Do you require a paper trail? Or do you rely on computers and electronic data?

5. How do you communicate with your friends and family while at school? Do you use the same method for everybody? Why or why not?

6. How can organizations ensure the ethical use of computer communications without eavesdropping on their employees' emails?

7. What kind of communication network does your family (or friends) use to plan get-togethers? How effective and efficient is it?

8. How often do you use the Internet? Is it a useful communication tool? What changes to you expect to see in the next decade?

9. In practice, how effective is your boss, teacher, or parent in their communications? What could he or she do to improve their communications?

10. Describe a cultural or gender communication problem you have encountered.

Chapter 15

Communication

Chapter Outline

I.   The Importance of Good Communication Skills

II. Communication and Management
    A.   The Importance of Good Communication
    B.   The Communication Process
        1.   Transmission phase
            a.   Verbal communication
            b.   Nonverbal communication
        2.   Feedback
    C.   The Role of Perception in Communication
    D.   The Dangers of Ineffective Communication

III. Information Richness and Communication Media
    A.   Face-to-Face Communication
    B.   Spoken Communication Electronically Communicated
    C.   Ethics In Action - Eavesdropping on Voice Mail
    D.   Personally Addressed Written Communication
    E.   Impersonal Written Communication

IV. Communication Networks
    A.   Communication Networks in Groups and Teams
        1.   Wheel network
        2.   Chain network
        3.   Circle network
        4.   All-channel network
    B.   Organizational Communication Networks

V.   Technological Advances in Communication
    A.   The Internet
    B.   Management Insight - Surfing the Net
    C.   Intranets
    D.   Management Insight - The Global Village
    E.   Groupware

VI. Communication Skills for Managers
    A.   Communication Skills for Managers as Senders
        1.   Send clear and complete messages

2.   Encode messages in symbols the receiver understands
3.   Select a medium appropriate for the message
4.   Select a medium that the receiver monitors
    a.   Focus on Diversity - Options in Communication Media for the Deaf
5.   Avoid filtering and information distortion
6.   Include a feedback mechanism in messages
7.   Provide accurate information
    a.   Management Insight - Communicating Accurate Information to Minimize Rumors

B.   Communication Skills for Managers as Receivers
1.   Pat attention
2.   Be a good listener
3.   Be empathetic

C.   Understanding Linguistic Styles
1.   Cross-cultural differences
2.   Gender differences
3.   Managing differences in linguistic styles

Study Questions

True - False Questions

____ 1.   Communication is the sharing of information between two or more individuals or groups to reach a common understanding.

____ 2.   Decoding is translating a message into understandable symbols or language.

____ 3.   Noise is anything that hampers the communication process.

____ 4.   The sender of an encoded message is called the medium.

____ 5.   An informal communication network along which unofficial information flows is referred to as the grapevine.

____ 6.   An intranet is a global system of computer networks.

____ 7.   Withholding part of a communication because one does not believe the receiver needs the information is called filtering.

____ 8.   Managers should try to change people's linguistic styles to fit the organization.

____ 9.   Communication occurs in a cyclical process that has two phases called encoding and decoding.

____ 10.   Intranets utilize the same technology as the Internet.

Multiple Choice Questions

_____ 1.   The person or group wishing to share information is known as the:
- A.   Medium
- B.   Receiver
- C.   Coder
- D.   Sender

_____ 2.   Anything that hampers any stage of the communication process is referred to as:
- A.   static.
- B.   noise.
- C.   buzz.
- D.   vibrations.

_____ 3.   Nonverbal communication includes the encoding of messages by means of:
- A.   Body language
- B.   Facial expressions
- C.   Styles of dress
- D.   All of the above

_____ 4.   Management by _____ is a face-to-face communication technique utilized by mangers to informally communicate with employees.
- A.   random walk
- B.   the grapevine
- C.   wandering around
- D.   walking around

_____ 5.   Computer software that enables members of groups or teams to share information with each other is called:
- A.   Groupware
- B.   Teamware
- C.   Intranets
- D.   Internet

_____ 6.   RAM. ROM, and CPU are examples of:
- A.   linguistic style
- B.   jargon
- C.   filtering
- D.   slang

_____ 7.   _____ changes the meaning of a message as the message passes through a series of senders and receivers.
- A.   Rumors
- B.   Linguistic styles

C.   Information distortions
D.   Filtering

8.   Communication occurs in a cyclical process that entails which phases:
              I.   Encoding
              II.   Decoding
              III. Transmission
              IV.   Feedback
      A.   III and IV
      B.   I and II
      C.   I, II, III, and IV
      D.   None of these

9.   Which of these is **not** a category of communication media:
      A.   Personally addressed written communication
      B.   Face-to-face communication
      C.   Confrontational written communication
      D.   Spoken communication electronically transmitted

10.   Communication media includes:
      A.   Voice mail
      B.   E-mail
      C.   Video conferences
      D.   All of these

11.   Which is a type of communication network?
              I.   Wheel
              II.   Spiral
              III. All-channel
              IV.   Channel
      A.   I and III
      B.   II and IV
      C.   I, II, and III
      D.   I, II, III, and IV

12.   Intranets are internal communication networks that managers can create to improve:
      A.   Performance
      B.   Communication
      C.   Customer service
      D.   All of these

13.   Managers should send messages that are all but which of these:
      A.   Clear and complete

B.   Encode messages in symbols that the sender understands
C.   Avoid filtering
D.   Choose a medium appropriate for the message

___ 14.   Communication skills for managers as receivers of messages does **not** include:
A.   Being a good listener
B.   Paying attention
C.   Being sympathetic
D.   Understanding linguistic styles

___ 15.   Linguistic styles can vary by:
I.   Gender
II.   Geographic region
III.   Culture

A.   I and III
B.   I, II, and III
C.   II and III
D.   I and III

Essay Questions

1.   What is the order of communication media, starting with the lowest information richness and progressing to the highest communication richness?

2.   Name the types of communication networks utilized by groups and teams.

3.   What communication skills should managers possess as senders of messages?

4.   Name three communication skills a manager should demonstrate to be a good receiver of messages.

Chapter 15
Communication

VIDEO EXERCISE
Communication and information technology is advancing at a rapid pace. AT&T has revealed its vision for revolutionizing work place communications in a futuristic style video. The impact of these advances will have a tremendous effect on the role of communication management in business.

The process of communications in organizations has been studied by management scholars for almost 100 years. The accumulation of knowledge in this important area of management is extensive. Yet, it is questionable whether much of it will apply as the new communications technologies take over the work place. After viewing the AT&T video, complete the following exercise.

PURPOSE:
To stimulate your thinking about current communication technologies, their direction, and the challenges they pose for managers.

PROCEDURE:
Identify one currently popular tool for communications in the workplace that was not widely available 20 years ago. Your task will be to examine how this device became popular in the workplace, the uses to which it has been put, and the new problems that it has created. Some examples of communications tools that have entered the workplace in the last 20 years are the fax machine, cellular telephones, computer networks, pagers, and voice mail. After you have identified the communications tool that interests you, write a briefing for class presentation that covers the following issues:

1.   When was the device invented? Often times new inventions take many years to disseminate and become widely used. Try to track down when the tool you are investigating was invented. Next, give a brief history of how the device came to its current rate of usage.

2.   How is the device currently being used in the workplace? Describe the primary and secondary uses to which the device has been put. What are its primary functions? Is it a money saver? A time saver? Has the device displaced any human workers? How do managers use the device to improve productivity, quality, and competitiveness?

3.   What new work place problems have been created by the device? Often, new tools for the work place are created to solve specific problems. Usually, the solution of those problems leads to new problems or issues. For example, the invention of the automobile was to solve the problem of travel, and it has led to the new problems of congestion and air pollution.

Journal Entries
Chapter 16 - Organizational Conflict, Politics and Change

Entry 22:
1. Do you tend to believe conflict is good or bad? Do you confront or avoid it?
2. What is the biggest source of conflict in your family? At school? At work?
3. Describe a situation you were in recently where you wee a successful (or unsuccessful) negotiator.
4. Have you ever been a victim of organizational politics? Have you ever used it to your advantage?
5. Have you tried to change recently? What factors influenced your ability to change?
6. How successful are you at making personal changes? What impacts your success or failure?
7. Has an organization you worked for tried to make a major change? Describe how it was attempted.

Chapter 16

Organizational Conflict, Negotiation, Politics, and Change

Chapter Outline

I.   The Power of Political Skills

II.   Organizational Conflict
     A.   Types of Conflict
         1.   Interpersonal conflict
         2.   Intragroup conflict
         3.   Intergroup conflict
         4.   Interorganizational conflict
     B.   Ethics In Action - Iacocca's Gamble
     C.   Sources of Conflict
         1.   Incompatible goals and time horizons
         2.   Overlapping authority
         3.   Task interdependencies
         4.   Incompatible evaluation or reward systems
         5.   Scarce resources
         6.   Status inconsistencies
     D.   Conflict Management Strategies
         1.   Strategies focused on individuals
              a.   Increasing awareness of the sources of conflict
              b.   Increasing diversity awareness and skills
              c.   Practicing job rotation or temporary assignments
              d.   Using permanent transfers or dismissals when necessary
         2.   Strategies focused on the whole organization
              a.   Changing an organization's structure or culture
              b.   Altering the source of conflict

III.   Negotiation Strategies for Integrative Bargaining
     A.   Emphasizing Subordinate Goals
     B.   Focusing on the Problem
     C.   Focusing on the Interests
     D.   Creating New Options for Joint Gain
     E.   Focusing on Fairness

IV.   Organizational Politics
     A.   The importance of Organizational Politics
     B.   Political Strategies for Increasing Power
         1.   Controlling uncertainty

146

2.   Making oneself irreplaceable
3.   Being in a central position
4.   Generating resources
5.   Building alliances
C.   Political Strategies for Exercising Power
1.   Relying on objective information
2.   Bringing in an outside expert
3.   Controlling the agenda
4.   Making everyone a winner

V.   Managing Organizational Change
A.   Assessing the Need for Change
B.   Deciding on the Change to Make
C.   Implementing the Change
D.   Evaluating the Change
E.   Management Insight - Big Changes at Tenneco

Study Questions

<u>True - False Questions</u>

___ 1.   Organizational conflict solely involves groups within organizations.

___ 2.   Adversarial negotiations in which parties compete to win the most resources while conceding as little as possible is known as distributive bargaining.

___ 3.   Top-down change is implemented gradually throughout the organization.

___ 4.   Bottom-up change is implemented quickly by employees at all levels of an organization.

___ 5.   Benchmarking compares performance on specific dimensions with the performance of high-performing organizations.

___ 6.   Four types of conflict that occur in organizations are interpersonal conflict, intragroup conflict, intergroup conflict, and interorganizational conflict.

___ 7.   Conflict strategies focused on the whole organization include changing an organization's structure or culture.

___ 8.   Negotiation is a conflict resolution technique used when parties in conflict that have disparate levels of power try to find an acceptable way to allocate resources.

___ 9.   Effective managers realize that politics can be a positive force.

147

____ 10.   Managing organizational change is one of managers' most important and difficult tasks.

Multiple Choice Questions

____ 1.   An adversarial negotiation in which parties compete to win the most resources without losing any resources is known as:
A.   distributive negotiation.
B.   distributive bargaining.
C.   distributive justice.
D.   integrative bargaining.

____ 2.   This is when parties work together in cooperative negotiation to achieve a positive resolution for all of the parties:
A.   Distributive negotiation
B.   Integrative bargaining
C.   Distributive bargaining
D.   Political bargaining

____ 3.   Activities that managers engage in to increase their power and to utilize their power more effectively to overcome their opposition is referred to as:
A.   Organizational politics
B.   Political strategies
C.   Integrative bargaining
D.   Power politics

____ 4.   _____ are tactics that managers use to increase their power and to use their power to gain support of other people while overcoming opposition.
A.   Organizational politics
B.   Political strategies
C.   Organizational strategies
D.   Top-down strategies

____ 5.   Goals that all parties in a conflict agree to are _____ goals.
A.   organizational
B.   integrative
C.   political
D.   superordinate

____ 6.   _____ change is implemented gradually and involves managers and employees at all levels of an organization.
A.   Linear
B.   Circular
C.   Bottom-up

D.   Top-down

___ 7.   Sources on conflict in an organization include:
          I.   Incompatible goals
          II.   Incompatible time horizons
          III.   Overlapping authority
          IV.   Task interdependence
    A.   I, II, III
    B.   II, III, IV
    C.   I, III, IV
    D.   I, II, III, IV

___ 8.   Sources or organizational conflict include all but which of these:
    A.   Incompatible evaluation systems
    B.   Consistent reward systems
    C.   Scarce resources
    D.   Status inconsistencies

___ 9.   In _____ negotiation, the parties perceive that there is a _____ level of resources
          for them to allocate, thus creating competition for the resources.
    A.   organizational; fixed
    B.   organizational; variable
    C.   distributive; fixed
    D.   distributive; variable

___ 10.   In ___ bargaining, the parties perceive they can increase the resource pie by
          creative solutions to the conflict.
    A.   integrative
    B.   distributive
    C.   initiative
    D.   interactive

___ 11.   Strategies that managers can use to facilitate integrative bargaining are to:
          I.   Emphasize organizational goals
          II.   Focus on the people
          III.   Focus on organizational demands
          IV.   Create new options for organizational gain
          V.   Focus on what is fair to the organization
    A.   I, II, III, IV, V
    B.   I, III, V
    C.   I, III, IV, V
    D.   None of these

___ 12.   Which is **not** a step in the organizational change process:
    A.   Deciding on the change to make

B. Assessing the need for change
C. Planning the change
D. Evaluating the success of the change

___ 13. Which of these is **not** a political strategy for increasing power:
A. Controlling the agenda
B. Being irreplaceable
C. Generating resources
D. Building alliances

___ 14. Which of the following is **not** a political strategy for exercising power:
A. Relying on objective information
B. Bringing in an outside expert
C. Controlling uncertainty
D. Making everyone a winner

___ 15. Which is **not** a type of organizational conflict?
A. Intrapersonal
B. Interpersonal
C. Intragroup
D. Intergroup

Essay Questions

1. What are the types of conflict in organizations?

2. Name the main sources of conflict in an organization.

3. What are the negotiation strategies for integrative bargaining?

4. Discuss the steps in the organizational change process.

Chapter 16
Organizational Conflict, Negotiation, Politics, and Change

Marshall Industries is one of the five largest distributors of industrial electronic components in America. From its expansive warehouses and corporate offices a few miles northeast of downtown Los Angeles, Marshall supplies 30,000 computer-related customers in the United States and Canada with a broad range of franchise brand name semiconductors, connectors, production supplies, and work stations. Marshall's stakeholders include its investors, more than 100 suppliers both domestic and international, and its staff and employees. Posted in highly visible work areas and on the back of their business cards is Marshall's mission statement. It reads: "Marshall Industries serves its business partners by adding value with a commitment to continuous improvement, innovation, and mutual satisfaction."

Marshall is a good example of how managers can successfully influence organizational systems, and how to implement change in corporate culture to improve quality and performance. In 1987 company founder Gordon Marshall came across a magazine article describing the benefits of a process called Total Quality Management. Marshall passed along the article to his President and Chief Operating Officer Robert Rodin. The Marshall Industry team, including Robert Rodin, president; Dick Bentley, executive vice president; Henry Chen, chief financial officer; Don Allero, vice president operation; Jacob Kuryan, director of quality; and others, changed the company's management style, technology, and organizational culture to better adapt to a changing business environment and growing international challenges. Within four years Marshall Industry's net income and stock value tripled.

How did Marshall manage such a dramatic turnaround? By applying some basic and some innovative management concepts.

To understand how successful managers change and affect a business, it's important to think of the entire organization as an interactive system where changing one sector can potentially affect several others. Robert Rodin, Marshall's president, said, "We see the business as very dependent. Each system in our company is very dependent on the next system. Our suppliers, our customers, and our internal customers' relationships have a tremendous dependency on one another. This requires everybody to work together like an orchestra or football team where each person has a job to do but no one job is more important than the other."

Virtually all business systems are dynamic. They shift and adapt to outside influences such as competitors, customer feedback, economic conditions, and public policies. Because they are open to external forces and are dynamic, organizational systems require managers to adapt their behavior to changing circumstances. Typically, within a matter of hours and sometimes minutes, managers shift their behavior between three categories of roles: interpersonal, informational, and decisional.

A manager is *interpersonal* when acting as a figurehead making an official appearance, when motivating and leading his or her staff, or when attempting to influence peers in other parts of the company.

An *informational* role most often revolves around the exchange of relevant information, such as monitoring the organization's output, disseminating information to staff members, and sharing company information with those outside and inside the organization.

A manager becomes *decisional* when he or she evaluates information and commits the organization to new directions. Real managerial success comes from integrating these three roles into seamless, flowing behavior everyday.

Rodin commented on the changes brought about at Marshall: "Our company has changed from focusing on results to looking at methods. We realized that by just looking at results we missed the content of the systems and processes that got us the results. And what we decided to do was look at those contents and make sure we were fixing the system and not just distorting it to get the results that we had forecast."

Managers must recognize how to move between different roles to effectively shape organizational behavior. To organize the clues that help them recognize and diagnose where, when, and how to make quality-oriented changes, managers often use mental models of the organizational system. One such model starts with the task or work at hand. How managers design tasks is crucial to employee motivation and productivity. Rodin noted how improved task design has affected employees at Marshall: "Our turnover is down, our absenteeism is down. We think there are many factors that contribute to that, not the least of which is that our people feel empowered. They know what is going on in their company. They have access to me, they have access to company strategies and the other leadership in the organization, and they are involved. I think that people feel proud of that. Often times we hear people bringing their families through to see the operation. And they take some real ownership in what the company is doing."

Technology can have a profound impact on changing the system. From the first assembly line robots to the latest fuzzy logic computers, changes in technology can assist in accomplishing a variety of tasks. Judith Formichella, vice president of MIS at Marshall, said, "The computer system change was necessary because there had not been a major upgrade to the system for probably 15 years. As you can imagine, in 15 years the business changed very dramatically. And because the technology was very old it was very cumbersome to manage and to make changes in order to respond quickly to business needs and business trends."

People are the fundamental elements of any organization. Managers have to decide who and how many employees to hire, train, and assign to certain tasks. Mike Lelo, warehouse manager, explained what he looks for in new hires: "I personally look for a person that hasn't necessarily worked in a warehouse before, but that has shown during the interview that they have some ambition, some goals, some dedication to their work. They are going to strive to do the best they possibly can regardless of what field of work they're in."

Organization is more than a flow chart in an employee manual. It's the structure and informational network that helps determine who makes what decisions that govern people's behavior at work. Robert Rodin described the changed culture at Marshall: "In the past, the company was clearly misaligned. Everybody was fighting with each other and there was no real teamwork because there wasn't the overarching mission that aligned everybody. In the new systems, the management team has developed a strategy we call the Marshall Process and that involves people, methods, material, and equipment. This allows us to use all aspects of the company to align itself for customer satisfaction."

Organizational culture involves people's fundamental assumptions about their values, beliefs, language, and rituals. These provide its members with guides to acceptable behavior. Corporate culture often expresses itself in the way new employees are taught how the company does things. Jacob Kuryan, director of quality, commented on how Marshall orients new employees: "In warehouse operations, for example, once they've gone through the orientation the new employee is assigned to an expert in the particular process area where they watch that expert work for two weeks. At the end of the two weeks the new employee gets tested on the process requirements. Once they pass the test they go back to work with the expert. Now the expert watches them perform the operation. Thus, when the employee has completed his training, he has a good understanding of what the requirements of the job is and how he fits into the big picture at Marshall."

Commitment to Total Quality Management is fundamental to Marshall's organizational culture of meeting and exceeding customer needs and expectations. As Robert Rodin, put it, 'We look at the people, the methods, the materials, the equipment, and the environment in solving the problems of the company as opposed to focusing solely on the result. In this way, we can truly find ways to add value to our customers. Once that's clearly defined to us we commit to continuous improvement and innovation so that we can go to new levels of excellence and customer satisfaction."

DISCUSSION QUESTIONS

1. How does an organization know when it's time for a change and why do employees frequently resist changes?

2. In order to implement change, the video stated that behavior must be "unfrozen, changed, and refrozen." What does this mean?

3. What is Force Field Analysis?

4. What are Red Letter Days at Marshall Industries?

5. How did Marshall's 500 sales representatives react to the Red Letter Day change of replacing the individualized incentive plan with a team approach to sales?

Journal Entries
Chapter 17 - Managing Information Systems and Technologies

Entry 23:
1. What data does your university gather for determining student admission?
2. How is that data transformed into useful information?
3. What data did you gather when determining which university to attend?
4. What technologies did you utilize to gather the useful information?
5. What technologies do you regularly use? What are your decision support systems?
6. How does your university control emerging technologies? Are they keeping up or falling behind?
7. How do computers and other communication technologies impact your workplace or home life?
8. What is your biggest fear and / or frustration regarding technology and our continuing reliance on it?
9. Describe how technological problems have impacted your efficiency and effectiveness.

Chapter 17

Managing Information Systems and Technologies

Chapter Outline

I. Information Flows at Tel Co. And Soft Co.

II. Information and the Manager's Job
- A. Attributes of Useful Information
  1. Quality
  2. Timeliness
  3. Completeness
  4. Relevance
- B. Information Systems Technology
- C. Information and Decisions
- D. Information and Control
- E. Management Insight - Information Systems and Control at Cypress Semiconductor
- F. Information and Coordination
- G. Managing Globally - Coordinating Global Production Flows at Bose Corporation

III. The Information Technology Revolution
- A. The Tumbling Price of Information
- B. Wireless Communications
- C. Computer Networks
- D. Software Developments
- E. Management Insights - IBM's Digital Factory

IV. Types of Management Information Systems
- A. The Organizational Hierarchy: The Traditional Information System
- B. Transition - Processing Systems
- C. Operations Information Systems
- D. Decision Support Systems
- E. Management Insight - How Judy Lewent Became One of the Most Powerful Women in Corporate America
- F. Expert Systems and Artificial Intelligence

V. The Impact and Limitations of Information Systems and Technology
- A. Information Systems and Organizational Structure
  1. Flattening organizations
  2. Horizontal information flows
- B. Information Systems and Competitive Advantage
- C. Management Insight - Levi's Personal Pair Made-to-Order Jeans

1.   Technological problems
2.   Resistence from individual users
3.   Political opposition
4.   Limitations of information systems
5.   Managing information systems

Study Questions

<u>True - False Questions</u>

___ 1.   Data is raw numbers organized in a meaningful fashion.

___ 2.   An information system is utilized for acquiring, organizing, storing, manipulating, and transmitting information.

___ 3.   Management information systems are systems that employees plan and design to provide themselves with the specific information they need.

___ 4.   The exchange of information through a group of interlinked computers is known as networking.

___ 5.   Software designed for a specific task or use is called designated software.

___ 6.   A transaction-processing system is designed to handle large volumes of routine, recurring transactions.

___ 7.   A sophisticated version of a decision support system that meets the need of upper-level managers is referred to as an executive support system.

___ 8.   An executive support system that links top managers so they can function as a team is called an expert system.

___ 9.   The system that employs human knowledge captured in a computer to solve problems is called an intelligence system.

___ 10.   Managers should emphasize that information systems are a substitute for face-to-face communication because they are more efficient.

<u>Multiple Choice Questions</u>

___ 1.   This is raw, un-summarized information:
A.   Data
B.   Informal information

C. Real-time information
D. Noisy information

___ 2. A _____ system is planned and designed by managers to provide themselves with the specific information they need.
A. real-time information
B. marketing information
C. management information
D. transition information

___ 3. This is an management information system designed to handle large volumes of routine, recurring transactions:
A. Applications-processing system
B. Transaction-processing system
C. Operations-processing system
D. Executive support system

___ 4. A(n) _____ system gathers, organizes, and summarizes comprehensive data in a form managers can use in their non-routine decision making tasks.
A. operations information
B. transaction-processing
C. decision support
D. executive support

___ 5. An interactive computer-based management information system that managers can use to make non-routine decisions is called a(n):
A. Operations information system
B. Decision support system
C. Executive support system
D. Transaction-processing system

___ 6. A sophisticated version of a decision support system that is designed for upper-level management is a(n) _____ support system.
A. decision
B. group decision
C. executive
D. officer

___ 7. The ____ support system is an executive support system that links top managers so they can function as a team.
A. team
B. executive
C. expert
D. group decision

___ 8. To build support for the introduction of new information systems, managers should create:

      I.   Backup support
      II.   Training programs
      III.   User-friendly systems

A.   I, II, III
B.   I and II
C.   II and III
D.   I and III

___ 9.   Properly implemented information systems can improve managers' ability to coordinate and control the organization's operations by providing managers with all but which of these types of information:

A.   Timely
B.   Relevant
C.   High-quality
D.   Complete

___ 10.   Information systems impact:

A.   Productivity
B.   Quality
C.   Responsiveness
D.   All of these

___ 11.   In recent year there have been rapid:

      I.   Advances in computing power
      II.   Declines in computer cost

A.   I
B.   II
C.   I and II
D.   Neither I nor II

___ 12.   Which of these has increased the potential for information technology to improve information systems:

      I.   Wireless communication
      II.   Falling prices
      III.   Software developments
      IV.   Computer networks

A.   I, III, IV
B.   I, II, III, IV
C.   II, III, IV
D.   I, III

___ 13.   Traditionally, managers have used the ___ hierarchy as a system for gathering

information they needed to make effective decisions.
A.   organizational
B.   static
C.   executive
D.   expert

___ 14.   Which of these is **not** a type of computer-based information systems used by managers:
A.   Transaction-processing
B.   Operations information
C.   Decision support
D.   Network

___ 15.   Problems in implementing information systems can arise from:

I.   Employees protecting their jobs
II.   Technology
III.   Employees protecting their power

A.   I, III
B.   II, III
C.   I, II, III
D.   I, II

Essay Questions

1.   Why can organizations be flatter with information systems?

2.   What are the factors affecting the usefulness of information?

3.   Moving from programmed to non-programmed decision making, what are the types of computer-based management information systems?

4.   What factors have increased the potential for information technology to increase efficacy?

Chapter 17
Managing Information and Technology

The World Wide Web is a fast-flowing river of information. Internet surfers have found that navigating the Web takes them to a wide range of sites from homemade personal sites to multimedia corporate site. Why are businesses willing to invest $200,00 to $1 million to create an impressive website? Some want to bolster their corporate image; others want to sell their product on-line.

How companies choose to reach out and hold their audiences' attention depends upon what they intend their sites to accomplish. Some websites function as general promotion and brand identity tools. For example, General Mills doesn't use its website to sell Betty Crocker cake mix, rather it uses the site to present menu plans and household tips. The goal is to link the brand's image with the information the website provides.

Another function of some business websites is to conduct on-line business (sometimes called on-line commerce, e-commerce, or transactional sites.) For example, you can book airline tickets on Sabre Group's Travelocity site; buy a computer on the Gateway 2000, Dell, and Micron sites; or buy stock from e.Schwab, Datek, and Quick & Reilly.

Unlike e-commerce sites, some brad-based corporate sites don't sell - they give things away. The aim of these sites is to give surfers easy access to huge banks of free information - particularly information about the companies' products. Microsoft is most likely the largest broad-based corporate site on the Web. The information about Microsoft products is so vast that the site changes about eight times a day as new information is added. Web designers have found that the better the website's organization, the more faith visitors have in the site's information and in the company. Corporate websites might contain information found in a brochure: description of products, phone numbers, addresses, email addresses, and so forth. They can also contain information that might be found in an annual report: shareholder information, corporate mission statements, company history, and press releases.

How companies use the Web, then, depends upon the type of company and on what the company wants their website to accomplish. On thing is certain, though, communication remains the main function of this new medium. People want answers to their questions and the Web can be the most efficient way to get them.

CRITICAL THINKING QUESTIONS
1. What are some of the ways companies are using the Intranet?

2. What are some of the ways companies are using the Internet?

3. Give an example of a specific company and its use of web sites.

Journal Entries
Chapter 18 - Managing Quality, Efficiency, and Responsiveness to Customers

Entry 24:
1. How did you define quality on your last big purchase?
2. What types of quality are you willing to pay extra for? What do you expect from any product or service?
3. Define your customers from work, or as you try to sell yourself to potential employers. What do your customers want?
4. How would you use TQM to improve your "job" as student?
5. Do you use a Just-in-time inventory system for your food, clothing, or studies? How does your inventory system work?
6. How would you redesign your house to improve efficiency?
7. How would you re-engineer the university to improve its customer service efficiency and effectiveness?

Chapter 18

Operations Management: Managing Quality, Efficiency, and Responsiveness to Customers

Chapter Outline

I.   Two Production Systems at Federal - Mogul

II.   Operations Management and Competitive Advantage

III. Improving Responsiveness to Customers
    A.   What Do Customers Want
    B.   Designing Production Systems That Are Responsive to Customers
    C.   Management Insight - How Southwest Airlines Keeps Its Customers Happy

IV.   Improving Quality
    A.   Total Quality Management
    B.   Management Insight - McDevitt Street Bovis Applies TQM
    C.   Putting TQM Into Action: The Management Challenge
        1.   Build organizational commitment to quality
        2.   Focus on the customer
        3.   Find ways to measure quality
        4.   Set goals and create incentives
        5.   Solicit input from employees
        6.   Identify defects and trace then to their sources
        7.   Introduce just-in-time inventory systems
            a.   Managing Globally - The *Kanban* System in Japan
        8.   Work closely with suppliers
        9.   Design for ease of manufacture
        10.   Break down barriers between functions
    D.   The Role of Top- and Functional-Level Managers in TQM

V.   Improving Efficiency
    A.   TQM and Efficiency
    B.   Facilities Layout, Flexible Manufacturing, and Efficiency
        1.   Product layout
        2.   Process layout
        3.   Fixed-position layout
    C.   Just-in-Time Inventory and Efficiency
    D.   Management Insight - Problems with JIT at GE Appliances
    E.   Self-Managed Work Teams and Efficiency
    F.   *Kaizen* and Efficiency

G. Managing Globally - Applying *Kaizen* to Improve Facilities Layout
H. Process Re-engineering and Efficiency
I. Management Insight - Re-engineering of Procurement at Ford
J. The Role of Top- and Functional-Level Managers in Efficiency

VI. Operations Management: Some Remaining Issues
A. Ethics In Action - The Human Cost of Improving Productivity

Study Questions

True - False Questions

___ 1. Operations management is management of any aspect of the production system that transforms inputs into finished goods and services.

___ 2. The system that an organization uses to acquire inputs, convert the inputs into outputs, and dispose of the outputs in called the production system.

___ 3. Inventory includes outputs in transit to a buyer.

___ 4. *Kaizen* is the Korean term for an all-embracing operations management philosophy that emphasizes the need for continuous improvement in the efficiency of an organization's production system.

___ 5. The fundamental rethinking and radical redesign of business processes to achieve dramatic improvements is referred to as process re-engineering.

___ 6. To achieve high performance in a competitive environment, it is imperative that the production system of an organization respond to customer demands.

___ 7. There are limits to how responsive an organization can be and still cover its costs.

___ 8. TQM requires a strong customer focus.

___ 9. Functional-level managers are responsible for setting the context within which efficiency improvements can take place.

___ 10. Top management bears the prime responsibility for identifying and implementing efficiency-enhancing improvements in production systems.

Multiple Choice Questions

___ 1. Groups of employees who meet regularly to discuss ways to increase quality are

called:
A. Managers
B. Quality circles
C. Production circles
D. Quality clusters

____ 2. In the _____ inventory system, supplies arrive to the organization when they are need, but not before then.
A. just-in-case
B. total quality
C. just-in-time
D. operations

____ 3. ____ manufacturing is an operations management technique that attempts to reduce the setup costs associated with a production system.
A. Flexible
B. Inflexible
C. Facilities
D. Feasible

____ 4. Process re-engineering redesigns processes to improvement measures of performance such as:
A. Cost
B. Quality
C. Speed
D. All of these

____ 5. To achieve high performance, managers try to improve their:
A. Customer responsiveness
B. Product quality
C. Organizational efficiency
D. All of these

____ 6. Which of these is **not** an improved production system?
A. Process re-engineering
B. Just-in-case delivery
C. TQM
D. *Kaizen*

____ 7. Managers seek to:
    I. Improve the quality of the outputs
    II. Lower production costs
    III. Lower prices
A. I and II
B. II and III

C.   I and III
D.   I, II, and III

___ 8.   Putting TQM into practice requires all but which of these:
A.   A strong customer focus
B.   Soliciting employee input
C.   Getting creditors to adopt TQM practices
D.   Breaking down barriers between functional departments

___ 9.   Improving efficiency requires all of these except:
A.   Adoption of flexible manufacturing technologies
B.   Institutionalization of a *Kanban* philosophy
C.   Establishment of self-managed work teams
D.   Process re-engineering

___ 10.   _____ managers bear prime responsibility for identifying and implementing efficiency-enhancing improvements in production systems.
A.   Functional-level
B.   Decision-level
C.   Top-level
D.   Organizational-level

___ 11   Which type of facilities layout is also known as mass production layout?
A.   Product layout
B.   Process layout
C.   Fixed-position layout
D.   Flexible layout

___ 12.   Which is **not** a type of facilities layout?
A.   Product
B.   Process
C.   Flexible
D.   Fixed-position

___ 13.   Which type of facilities layout has relatively self-contained work stations?
A.   Product
B.   Process
C.   Flexible
D.   Fixed-position

___ 14.   Self-managed teams use this type of facilities layout:
A.   Product
B.   Process
C.   Fixed-position
D.   Flexible

_____ 15.   This type of facilities layout is utilized for production of jet airliners and mainframe computers:
        A.   Process
        B.   Product
        C.   Flexible
        D.   Fixed-position

Essay Questions

1.   What are the types of facilities layouts?

2.   Which type of facilities layout would typically be utilized for production of large or difficult to assemble products?

3.   Discuss the impact of increased quality on organizational performance.

4.   What are the three stages of the production system, and what is used or produced in each stage?

Chapter 18
Operations Management: Managing Quality, Efficiency, and Responsiveness to Customers

A poorly scheduled job breeds chaos. In business, workflow equals cash flow, and workflow is driven by the schedule. In an ideal situation the schedule is followed, jobs are completed on time, the shop stays busy, and the pace remains steady. But what if changes need to be made at a moment's notice? What if a special order needs to be filled quickly? What if extra time is needed to set up a special job? All of these factors change the schedule whether you're producing bicycles, bagels, bass guitars, or bank statements. Effective production scheduling will make a company more competitive. The successful job shop is one that is designed to handle changes quickly and without loss of time of disruption to the operation.

Washburn Guitars produces 115,000 instruments annually. These range from acoustic and electric guitars and basses to mandolins and banjos. At its Chicago plant, Washburn produces about 15 top-of-the-line electric guitars each day. Its instruments are played by musicians like David Gilmore of Pink Floyd, Joe Parry of Arrowsmith, Darryl Smith of the Rolling Stones, Graham Parker, and Gregg Allman.

Grover Jackson, a world-renowned guitar designer, oversees operations at the Chicago plant. The production process at Washburn might be described as a *synthetic* system. This means that the materials used to build each guitar undergo many physical changes from start to finish. Scheduling each of these operations is important to ensure that there's an even flow through production, with minimum bottleneck occurring and with the numbers of each model to meet demand.

Production schedules vary from nearly continuous batches all the way down to custom, special order, and one-of-a-kind instruments. Collectively this process could be called *intermittent process,* meaning the production runs are short and the machines are changed frequently to produce different pieces.

Sometimes scheduling can be affected by *priority rules.* Scheduling priority may be based on such criteria as first come first served, earliest due date, and shortest operating time. For example, at Washburn, the production of a popular, more expensive guitar may take precedence over the manufacturing schedule of a less expensive item.

Another prioritizing factor relates to the length of time needed to produce a given guitar model. Occasionally Washburn gets rush orders from big-name musicians on concert tours. Brady Breen, Washburn's production/facilities manager, said, "Very often a musician will need a piece at the drop of a hat. If it's been stolen we need to replace those. If it's been broken and it's repairable they send it to us and we repair it. If it's not, we need to build them another one to keep the artist with his instrument."

Since manufacturing different guitar components for a variety of models requires frequent new setups of critical machinery, scheduling work is important at Washburn. The company uses a system known as *flexible* manufacturing since the production machine can perform multiple tasks or jobs, and can produce a variety of products. The same machine builds guitar necks, drills holes for the fret board, body, and electronics, and handles this task for a variety of different models.

The production of an electric guitar begins with the gluing and shaping of the wood to make the guitar's body Next, the hardware and electronics components are assembled. This consists of pick ups, tuning keys, the bridge, wiring, and strings. Everything is tested at the point of assembly before it is shipped.

The rotation and availability of parts in stock can also affect production scheduling. At Washburn it generally takes 90 days to purchase the parts for a new model. The introduction of a new model means new parts and new production specifications. Currently, Washburn produces its line of acoustic guitars overseas. But there are plans to move the entire production operation, acoustic and electric, to a new 120,000-square-foot facility in Nashville, Tennessee. Breen explained, "In an effort to expand our existing production there have been considerations to move to Nashville where we would have the liberty of building a larger structure customized to our specifications and take advantage of the labor pool, which is considered to be the center of the guitar making industry."

Today more information systems are available than ever before and new production technologies are being developed at a fast pace. Managers of the future will need to have a strong knowledge of the links between the scheduling of work, the production process, and how they impact market demand and customer satisfaction. The company with the most effective production schedule is going to be better able to provide the customer with the right product at the right time for the right place. So whether you're making cars, computers, copiers, or cheeseburgers, good scheduling will make a big difference in the success of your business.

DISCUSSIONS QUESTIONS

1. Define what is meant by "priority rules." What are some possible priority rules at Washburn?

2. Define flexible manufacturing. How does it differ from traditional assembly line manufacturing?

3. What are some of the ways in which information technologies have changed manufacturing? In what ways have manufacturing jobs changed?

Journal Entries
Chapter 19 - The Management of Innovation, Product Development, and Entrepreneurship

Entry 25:
1. Do you prefer incremental or quantum changes? Explain.
2. Where are you at in terms of your product life cycle?
3. What is your favorite new product? How do you think it was invented?
4. What do you wish somebody would invent to make your life easier? Have you ever considered doing it?
5. Would you describe yourself as an entrepreneur? Why or Why not?
6. Do you know a successful or unsuccessful entrepreneur? What factors impacted his or her success?
7. Did the organization you work(ed) for value entrepreneurship? Cite an example.

Chapter 19

The Management of Innovation, Product Development, and Entrepreneurship

Chapter Outline

I.   Two Product Development Teams at Quantum Corporation

II.   Innovation, Technological Change, and Competition
    A.   The Effects of Technological Change
    B.   Product Life Cycles and Product Development
        1.   The rate of technological change
        2.   The role of fads and fashion
        3.   Managerial implications
    C.   Management Insight - Shrinking Product Life Cycles at Intel

III.   Product Development
    A.   Goals of Product Development
        1.   Reducing development time
            a.   Management Insight - How Sun Captured the Lead From Apollo
        2.   Maximizing the fit with customer needs
        3.   Maximizing product quality
        4.   Maximizing manufacturability and efficiency
    B.   Principles of Product Development
        1.   Management Insight - How Thermos Developed a New Barbecue Grill
        2.   Establish a stage-gate development funnel
        3.   Establish cross-functional teams
        4.   Use concurrent engineering
        5.   Involve both customers and suppliers
            a.   Management Insight - Developing the 777 at Boeing
    C.   Problems with Product Development
    D.   Managing Globally - Ford's Attempt at Global Product Development

IV.   Entrepreneurship
    A.   Entrepreneurship and New Ventures
        1.   Characteristics of entrepreneurs
        2.   Entrepreneurship and management
        3.   Developing a plan for a new business
    B.   Intrapreneurship and Organizational Learning
        1.   Product champions
        2.   Skunkworks and new venture divisions
        3.   Rewards for innovation

Study Questions

____ 1.   Concurrent engineering is simultaneous design of a product and of the process for marketing the product.

____ 2.   An intrapreneur is one who notices opportunities and takes responsibility for improved goods and services.

____ 3.   A manager who seeks ownership of s project and provides leadership that take a product from the idea stage to the customer is called a core member.

____ 4.   A skunkworks is a group of intrapreneurs who are deliberately separated from the normal operations of an organization.

____ 5.   The term "skunkworks" was coined at Lockheed Corporation.

____ 6.   Increasingly, companies are rewarding intrapreneurs on the basis of outcomes from the product development process.

____ 7.   A new venture division's managers become intrapreneurs in charge of product development.

____ 8.   Rapid technological change usually can shorten product life cycles.

____ 9.   Entrepreneurs find new ventures on their own, while intrapreneurs work inside an organization to manage the product development process.

____ 10.   Organizations need to discourage intrapreneurship because it leads to organizational changes.

Multiple Choice Questions

____ 1.   A fundamental shift in technology that results in the innovation of new kinds of goods and services is called:
            A.   Quantum technological change
            B.   Incremental technological change
            C.   Quantum product innovations
            D.   Incremental product innovations

____ 2.   _____ is change that refines existing technology and leads to gradual improvements over time.
            A.   Quantum technological change

B.   Incremental technological change
C.   Product technological change
D.   Spatial technological change

___ 3.   Which of these rarely occurs:
                        I.   Incremental product innovations
                        II.   Quantum product innovations
A.   I
B.   II
C.   Both I and II
D.   Neither I nor II

___ 4.   Car model changes are an example of _____ product innovations.
A.   quantum
B.   spatial
C.   incremental
D.   None of these is correct

___ 5.   What is the correct order of the product life cycle?
                        I.   Embryonic
                        II.   Growth
                        III.   Maturity
                        IV.   Decline
A.   I, II, III, IV
B.   II, I, III, IV
C.   IV, III, II, I.
D.   II, III, IV

___ 6.   The _____ development funnel is a model that forces managers to choose among competing projects.
A.   star-gate
B.   stage-gate
C.   funnel-gate
D.   flood-gate

___ 7.   The stage-gate development funnel begins with a ___ mouth.
A.   shut
B.   narrow
C.   wide
D.   closed

___ 8.   A contract book details product development factors such as:
                        I.   Resource commitments
                        II.   Development milestones
                        III.   Time lines

A.   I and III
B.   II and III
C.   I and II
D.   I, II, and III

___ 9.   "Skunkworks" was coined at:
A.   Lockheed Corporation
B.   Microsoft
C.   Cisco Systems
D.   PepsiCo

___ 10.   The ____ division is given all the resources it needs to develop and market a new product.
A.   concurrent
B.   quantum
C.   new venture
D.   stage-gate

___ 11.   Large organizations can become:
                    I.   Tall
                    II.   Flexible
                    III.   Bureaucratic
A.   I, II, III
B.   II and III
C.   I and II
D.   I and III

___ 12.   Which is **not** a principle of product development?
A.   Establish a stage-gate development funnel
B.   Establish cross-functional teams
C.   Use sequential engineering
D.   Involve customers and suppliers in the development process

___ 13.   Which of these is **not** a stage in a product's life cycle:
A.   Embryonic
B.   Zygote
C.   Maturity
D.   Decline

___ 14.   Which is **not** a goal of new product development:
A.   Maximize development time
B.   Maximize quality
C.   Maximize efficiency
D.   Maximize the fit with customer needs

_____ 15.   Which is a stage in the parallel development process?

                                     I.   Opportunity identification
                                     II.   Product design
                                     III.   Process design
                                     IV.   Commercial production

        A.   I, II, III, IV
        B.   II, III, IV
        C.   I, II, IV
        D.   I, III, IV

Essay Questions

1. What are the stages of a product life cycle, and what does the level of demand do in each one?

2. Name the four goals of new product development.

3. Distinguish sequential product development from partly parallel product development.

4. What are the stages in developing a business plan?

Journal Entries
Concluding Entry

To conclude your journal, write one last "comprehensive" entry. This entry should be a summary of what you learned from this class by keeping the journal. This is not a request for a list of terms and definitions, but rather a request for your insight on the usefulness and application of the material we discussed. Topics to address (entry ideas) include:

1. What was the most useful topic for you - currently, or anticipated in the future?
2. What was the most surprising thing you learned/applied?
3. What do you wish we would have covered in more depth?
4. What do you wish we would have covered, but didn't?
5. What insights into management will you remember a year, five years, or ten years from now?

Answers to the Study Questions

Answers
to the
Study Questions

Chapter 1

True - False Questions

1. T
2. F
3. F
4. F
5. F
6. T
7. T
8. F
9. T
10. T

Multiple Choice Questions

1. A
2. A
3. D
4. B
5. B
6. C
7. C
8. B
9. D
10. B
11. A
12. C
13. A
14. D
15. C

Essay Questions

1. Because strategies are not always immediately clear; therefore, managers take risks when they commit resources to pursue a strategy.

2. Managers articulate a clear vision, energize the workforce, and enable employees to understand the part they play in achieving organizational goals.

3. Dell's company grew so rapidly it was difficult to establish the need systems, and he had no experienced managers to help him.

4. Build a competitive advantage, be responsive to customers, to act ethically toward everyone, manage a diverse workforce, and utilize new technology and information systems.

Chapter 2

True - False Questions

1. T
2. T
3. T
4. F
5. F

Multiple Choice Questions

1. B
2. A
3. C
4. D
5. A

6.	T		6.	A
7.	T		7.	B
8.	F		8.	C
9.	F		9.	D
10.	F		10.	B
			11.	D
			12.	C
			13.	D
			14.	A
			15.	C

Essay Questions

1. Esprit de corps is valuable because employees who are enthusiastic and enjoy being part of a group are more productive and satisfied.

2. Theory X assumes workers are lazy and thus a manager must supervise them closely or they will not be productive. Theory Y has positive assumptions that leads a manager to try to create an encouraging work environment that allows employees to take the initiative.

3. Unity of command states that an employee should receive orders from only one supervisor. If two or more exist, crossed lines of communication and authority will decrease productivity and lead to decreased job satisfaction.

4. Long-term employees have developed the necessary skills to improve a business. They should be more efficient and effective.

Chapter 3

True - False Questions			Multiple Choice Questions	
1.	F		1.	A
2.	T		2.	B
3.	T		3.	D
4.	F		4.	B
5.	F		5.	A
6.	T		6.	B
7.	F		7.	D
8.	F		8.	C
9.	T		9.	B
10.	T		10.	C
			11.	A
			12.	D
			13.	D
			14.	A
			15.	C

1.   The two components are the task environment (forces from suppliers, customers, distributors, and competitors) and the general environment (factors that affect the organization and its task environment).

2.   Compliance avoids bad press and civil and criminal punishment for the organization and the managers, while enhancing the public's perception of the organization.

3.   It is developed by building departmental skills and resources, empowering managers, and choosing a mechanistic or organic structure.

4.   Such activities as representing and protecting the organization, gatekeeping, information processing, and establishing interorganizational relationships.

Chapter 4

True - False Questions		Multiple Choice Questions	
1.	F	1.	B
2.	T	2.	D
3.	F	3.	A
4.	T	4.	C
5.	F	5.	A
6.	F	6.	B
7.	T	7.	D
8.	T	8.	C
9.	F	9.	A
10.	F	10.	C
		11.	B
		12.	B
		13.	C
		14.	D
		15.	A

Essay Questions
1.   Governmental (such as tariffs and import quotas) and self-imposed impediments (such as ethical standards).

2.   The forces are competitors, suppliers, customers, and distributors.

3.   The political and legal systems, the socio-cultural systems, and the economic systems.

4.   From highest to lowest levels of foreign involvement, the four ways are a wholly-owned foreign subsidiary, strategic alliances and joint ventures, licensing and franchising, and importing and exporting.

Chapter 5

True - False Questions		Multiple Choice Questions	
1.	T	1.	D
2.	F	2.	C
3.	F	3.	D
4.	T	4.	A
5.	F	5.	A
6.	F	6.	C
7.	F	7.	B
8.	F	8.	D
9.	F	9.	A
10.	T	10.	A
		11.	B
		12.	C
		13.	A
		14.	D
		15.	B

Essay Questions

1. The sources for the codes of ethics are societal ethics, professional ethics, and individual ethics (of the organization's employees).

2. Provide workers with the opportunity to enhance their skills and education, contribute to charities, allow workers time off for family or health situations, and keeping a business in the same location to benefit the workers and the community.

3. From lowest to highest, the approaches are the obstructionist approach, defensive approach, accommodative approach, and the pro-active approach.

4. Disabilities, age, gender, race, ethnicity, religion, socio-economic background, and sexual orientation.

Chapter 6

True - False Questions		Multiple Choice Questions	
1.	T	1.	B
2.	T	2.	B
3.	F	3.	A
4.	T	4.	C
5.	T	5.	B
6.	T	6.	A
7.	F	7.	B
8.	F	8.	C
9.	F	9.	D
10.	F	10.	A

11.	B
12.	B
13.	B
14.	D
15.	C

Essay Questions
1.   Listing the alternatives and consequences of alternatives, ranking each alternative from least to most preferred, and selecting the alternative that leads to the desired future consequences.

2.   Information is incomplete due to uncertainty and risk, ambiguous information and time constraints, and information costs.

3.   Recognize the need for a decision, generate alternatives, assess the alternatives, choose among the alternatives, implement the chosen one, and learn from feedback.

4.   1) Develop personal mastery; 2) build complex and challenging mental models; 3) promote team learning; 4) build shared vision; and 5) encourage systems thinking.

Chapter 7

True - False Questions

1.	F
2.	F
3.	F
4.	T
5.	F
6.	F
7.	T
8.	T
9.	T
10.	T

Multiple Choice Questions

1.	C
2.	C
3.	A
4.	D
5.	B
6.	A
7.	B
8.	A
9.	C
10.	D
11.	B
12.	C
13.	B
14.	C
15.	A

Essay Questions
1.   The three steps are determining the organizations's mission and goals, formulating strategy, and implementing strategy.

2.   SWOT is strengths, weaknesses, opportunities, and threats. It is useful to determine the current of the organization, plan a strategy for the opportunities, and avoid the threats.

3.	Corporate-level strategies are strategies such as concentration on a single business, diversification, international expansion, and vertical integration.

4.	1) Allocate responsibilities, 2) draft detailed action plans, 3) establish a time table for implementation, 4) allocate appropriate resources, and 5) hold individuals and groups accountable for attaining goals.

Chapter 8

True - False Questions		Multiple Choice Questions	
1.	F	1.	D
2.	F	2.	C
3.	T	3.	D
4.	T	4.	D
5.	F	5.	A
6.	F	6.	B
7.	F	7.	B
8.	T	8.	A
9.	F	9.	C
10.	F	10.	A
		11.	B
		12.	C
		13.	D
		14.	B
		15.	D

Essay Questions

1.	When managers enter into a series of strategic alliances with other organizations, and a substantial number of activities are performed outside of the organization, they have created a network structure.

2.	The factors that affect organizational structure are the organizational environment, technology, human resources, and strategy.

3.	The job characteristics are skill variety, task identity, task significance, autonomy, and feedback.

4.	Direct contact, liaison roles, task forces, cross-functional teams, integrating roles and departments, and matrix structures.

Chapter 9

True - False Questions		Multiple Choice Questions	
1.	F	1.	A
2.	F	2.	B

3.	T		3.	D
4.	F		4.	A
5.	F		5.	C
6.	F		6.	B
7.	F		7.	A
8.	F		8.	C
9.	F		9.	C
10.	T		10.	B
			11.	C
			12.	D
			13.	A
			14.	C
			15.	B

Essay Questions

1. The input stage utilizes feedforward control, the conversion stage uses concurrent control, and the output stage uses feedback control.

2. Establish standards of performance and goals against which performance will be evaluated; measure actual performance; compare actual performance against the chosen standards of performance; and, evaluate the result and initiate corrective action if necessary.

3. Financial measures of performance, organizational goals, and operating budgets.

4. The factors are values of the founder, ceremonies and rites, stories and language, and socialization.

Chapter 10

True - False Questions		Multiple Choice Questions	
1.	T	1.	C
2.	F	2.	B
3.	F	3.	A
4.	F	4.	D
5.	F	5.	B
6.	F	6.	A
7.	F	7.	D
8.	T	8.	A
9.	T	9.	C
10.	T	10.	B
		11.	A
		12.	D
		13.	A
		14.	D
		15.	B

1.   The components are recruitment and solicitation, training and development, performance appraisal and feedback, pay and benefits, and labor relations.

2.   The tools for selection are background information, references, paper-and-pencil tests, physical ability tests, performance tests, and interviews.

3.   Job analysis identifies the tasks, duties, and responsibilities of the job, and the knowledge, skills, and abilities necessary to do the job.

4.   Supervisors, customers/clients, subordinates, self, and peers.

Chapter 11

True - False Questions		Multiple Choice Questions	
1.	T	1.	C
2.	F	2.	B
3.	F	3.	B
4.	T	4.	A
5.	F	5.	C
6.	T	6.	D
7.	F	7.	A
8.	F	8.	B
9.	T	9.	C
10.	F	10.	D
		11.	A
		12.	C
		13.	B
		14.	D
		15.	D

Essay Questions
1.   The big five are extroversion, negative affectivity, agreeableness, conscientiousness, and openness to experiences.

2.   Positive mood measures are moods such as active, strong, excited, enthusiastic, peppy, and elated.

3.   A linear career move progresses from preparation for work, to organizational entry, to early career, to mid-career, to late career.

4.   Positive stress raises a manager's performance to do his or her best from a low beginning, while negative stress paralyzes a manager and causes his or her performance to fall form a higher level to a much lower level.

Chapter 12

True - False Questions		Multiple Choice Questions	
1.	T	1.	D
2.	T	2.	B
3.	F	3.	C
4.	T	4.	A
5.	F	5.	B
6.	F	6.	A
7.	T	7.	B
8.	F	8.	C
9.	F	9.	D
10.	T	10.	C
		11.	A
		12.	D
		13.	A
		14.	D
		15.	D

Essay Questions

1.   Expectancy is a person's perception about the extent to which his or her effort will result in a certain level of performance. Instrumentality is a person's perception about the extent that performance at a certain level will result in the attainment of outcomes. Valence is how desirable and available outcome is to a person.

2.   High motivation is expectancy theory is achieved when expectancy, instrumentality, and valence are all high.

3.   Psychological, safety, belongingness, esteem, and self-actualization.

4.   Existence needs, relatedness needs, and growth needs.

Chapter 13

True - False Questions		Multiple Choice Questions	
1.	T	1.	A
2.	F	2.	A
3.	T	3.	D
4.	T	4.	B
5.	F	5.	C
6.	F	6.	A
7.	T	7.	B
8.	T	8.	C
9.	T	9.	D

10.	F		10.	C
			11.	B
			12.	D
			13.	A
			14.	B
			15.	C

Essay Questions

1. Effective leadership is contingent on the nature of the subordinates and the work that they do.

2. Whether or not leadership is necessary for subordinates to perform is highly contingent on characteristics of the subordinates and the situation.

3. Transformational managers are charismatic, they intellectually stimulate subordinates, and they engage in developmental consideration.

4. Effective leaders exhibit, among other traits, the following traits: intelligence, knowledge and expertise, dominance, self-confidence, high energy, tolerance for stress, integrity and honesty, and maturity.

Chapter 14

True - False Questions		Multiple Choice Questions	
1.	T	1.	B
2.	F	2.	A
3.	F	3.	D
4.	F	4.	C
5.	F	5.	B
6.	T	6.	A
7.	T	7.	C
8.	F	8.	D
9.	T	9.	A
10.	T	10.	B
		11.	C
		12.	C
		13.	A
		14.	D
		15.	B

Essay Questions

1. The contributions are enhanced performance, increased customer responsiveness, increased innovation, and increased motivation and satisfaction.

2. The five stages are forming, storming, norming, performing, and adjourning.

3. The factors are group size, effectively managed diversity, group identity and healthy competition, and success.

4. Make individual group contributions identifiable, emphasize the value of contributions by individual members, and keep group size at an appropriate level.

Chapter 15

True - False Questions

1. T
2. F
3. T
4. F
5. T
6. F
7. T
8. F
9. F
10. T

Multiple Choice Questions

1. D
2. B
3. D
4. C
5. A
6. B
7. C
8. A
9. C
10. D
11. A
12. D
13. B
14. C
15. B

Essay Questions

1. The lowest is impersonal written communication, then personally addressed written communication, spoken communication electronically transmitted, and then face-to-face communication.

2. The communication networks are the wheel, chain, circle, and all-channel networks.

3. Seven skills: clear and complete messages, encode in symbols that the receiver understands, use an appropriate medium, select a medium the receiver monitors, avoid filtering and distorting, utilize a feedback mechanism, and provide accurate information to stop the spread of rumors.

4. Manager as a receiver: pay attention, be a good listener, and be empathetic.

Chapter 16

True - False Questions

1. F
2. F

Multiple Choice Questions

1. A
2. B

3.	F		3.	A
4.	F		4.	B
5.	T		5.	D
6.	T		6.	C
7.	T		7.	D
8.	F		8.	B
9.	T		9.	C
10.	T		10.	A
			11.	D
			12.	C
			13.	A
			14.	C
			15.	A

Essay Questions

1.   The types of organization conflicts are interpersonal, intragroup, intergroup, and interorganizational conflicts.

2.   Sources of conflict include incompatible goals and time horizons, overlapping authority, task interdependence, incompatible evaluation reward systems, scarce resources, and status inconsistencies.

3.   Emphasize superordinate goals, focus on the problem and not the people, focus on interests not demands, create new options for joint gain, and focus on what is fair.

4.   Assess the need for change (recognize and identify the problem), decide to make the change (organization's future), implement the change (how to do it), and evaluate the change (benchmarking).

Chapter 17

True - False Questions			Multiple Choice Questions	
1.	F		1.	A
2.	T		2.	C
3.	F		3.	B
4.	T		4.	A
5.	F		5.	B
6.	T		6.	C
7.	T		7.	D
8.	F		8.	A
9.	F		9.	D
10.	F		10.	D
			11.	C
			12.	B
			13.	A

Essay Questions

1. Organizations can be flatter due to utilization of the information systems to encourage more lateral cross-functional (rather than more top-to-bottom) communication.

2. The factors are quality, timeliness, completeness, and relevance.

3. Transaction-processing systems, operations information systems, decision support systems, and expert systems.

4. Falling prices, wireless communication, computer networks, and software developments.

Chapter 18

True - False Questions		Multiple Choice Questions	
1.	T	1.	B
2.	T	2.	C
3.	F	3.	A
4.	F	4.	D
5.	T	5.	D
6.	T	6.	B
7.	T	7.	A
8.	T	8.	C
9.	F	9.	B
10.	F	10.	A
		11.	A
		12.	C
		13.	B
		14.	C
		15.	D

Essay Questions

1. Product layout, process layout, and fixed-position layout.

2. Fixed-position layout would be used so each (usually) self-managed team will move to the large or complex product being produced.

3. Increased quality will either increase reliability leading to higher prices and higher profits, or it will increase productivity which will lead to lower costs and higher profits.

4. The input stage uses raw materials, component parts, and labor. The conversion stage uses skills, machines, and computers. The output stage produces goods and services.

Chapter 19

<table>
<tr><td colspan="2">True - False Questions</td><td colspan="2">Multiple Choice Questions</td></tr>
<tr><td>1.</td><td>F</td><td>1.</td><td>A</td></tr>
<tr><td>2.</td><td>T</td><td>2.</td><td>B</td></tr>
<tr><td>3.</td><td>F</td><td>3.</td><td>B</td></tr>
<tr><td>4.</td><td>T</td><td>4.</td><td>C</td></tr>
<tr><td>5.</td><td>T</td><td>5.</td><td>A</td></tr>
<tr><td>6.</td><td>T</td><td>6.</td><td>B</td></tr>
<tr><td>7.</td><td>T</td><td>7.</td><td>C</td></tr>
<tr><td>8.</td><td>T</td><td>8.</td><td>D</td></tr>
<tr><td>9.</td><td>T</td><td>9.</td><td>A</td></tr>
<tr><td>10.</td><td>F</td><td>10.</td><td>C</td></tr>
<tr><td></td><td></td><td>11.</td><td>D</td></tr>
<tr><td></td><td></td><td>12.</td><td>C</td></tr>
<tr><td></td><td></td><td>13.</td><td>B</td></tr>
<tr><td></td><td></td><td>14.</td><td>A</td></tr>
<tr><td></td><td></td><td>15.</td><td>A</td></tr>
</table>

Essay Questions

1. Embryonic stage (zero to slowly rising demand), the growth stage (big increase), the maturity stage (increase, levels off, then begins to decline), and the decline stage (declines throughout this stage).

2. Reduce development time, maximize fit with customer needs, maximize manufacturability and efficiency, and maximize product quality.

3. Sequential product development takes the five stages (opportunity identification, concept development, product design, process design, and commercial production) in order, while partly parallel product development has somewhat overlapping stages (one stage overlaps into the next stage).

4. Four steps are notice a product opportunity and develop a basic business idea; conduct a SWOT analysis; decide if the opportunity is feasible; and, prepare a detailed business plan.